MW00606611

Endorsements for *Bring It To Life*

Christian educators are concerned with spiritual formation; that is, students changed in how they think, feel, live, and love through what they learn. Swaner and Erdvig provide Christian school educators an intensely pragmatic, step-by-step process for implementing service-learning—and uniquely, in a distinctively-biblical context, demonstrating how it can be used to foster personal Christ-likeness, shape one's worldview, reveal God's calling on one's life, and serve as an act of worship. This is a must-have resource for every Christian school educator who wants to teach for transformation.

> —*Jay Ferguson, PhD, Head of School, Grace Community School*

Swaner and Erdvig offer a helpful way forward for Christian educators to redefine true service-learning from a biblical perspective, and to enliven, engage, and connect students to meaningful work serving others. Excellent real-life examples inspire the reader, helpful end-of-chapter questions guide the reader into action, and a comprehensive assessment section demystifies data gathering. It is a must read for anyone interested in deepening student engagement and lifetime learning in Christian schools!

> —*Dan Beerens, Educational Consultant, CACE Fellow*

I believe that if the practices outlined in this book were implemented in every classroom, service-learning would become the foremost character building program for a young heart and mind. Service-learning has taken the focus off "self" for my students and redirected it toward others, inevitably resulting in gratitude and a sensitivity to others' needs. Service-learning has inspired me to think and teach more creatively, and I'm convinced I'm intentionally developing the selfless leaders of tomorrow.

> —*Taryn Martin, Fourth Grade Teacher, Smithtown Christian School*

Bring It To Life:

Christian Education and the Transformative Power of Service-Learning

Lynn E. Swaner
Roger C. S. Erdvig

© 2018 by ACSI

All rights reserved. No portion of this book may be reproduced, stored in a retrieval system, or transmitted, in any form or by any means—mechanical, photocopying, recording, or otherwise—without prior written permission of ACSI.

The Association of Christian Schools International (ACSI) is committed to the ministry of Christian school education, to enable Christian educators and schools worldwide to effectively prepare students for life. ACSI strives to produce biblically sound materials that reflect Christian scholarship and stewardship and that address the identified needs of Christian schools around the world.

Views expressed in this book are those of the authors, and do not necessarily represent the views or the position of the Association of Christian Schools International.

Unless otherwise identified, all Scriptures are taken from the THE HOLY BIBLE, ENGLISH STANDARD VERSION (ESV): Scriptures taken from THE HOLY BIBLE, ENGLISH STANDARD VERSION ® Copyright© 2001 by Crossway, a publishing ministry of Good News Publishers. Used by permission.

The K–12 Service-Learning Standards for Quality Practice (National Youth Leadership Council 2008) are reprinted with permission of the copyright holder.

Printed in the United States of America

23 22 21 20 19 18   1 2 3 4 5 6 7

Swaner, Lynn E., and Roger C. S. Erdvig
Bring It To Life:
Christian Education and the Transformative Power of Service-Learning
ISBN   978-1-58331-558-3 Catalog # 6675
eISBN 978-1-58331-513-2 Catalog # e6675

Editor: John Conaway
Association of Christian Schools International
731 Chapel Hills Drive • Colorado Springs, CO 80920
Member Care: 800.367.0798 • www.acsi.org

Contents

Author Bios

Dr. Lynn E. Swaner is the Director of Thought Leadership at ACSI, where she leads initiatives to address compelling challenges and opportunities facing Christian education. Prior to joining ACSI she served as a Christian school administrator and a graduate professor of education. A published scholar and conference speaker, her focus is on engaged pedagogy and creating cultures that foster student learning. She received her EdD from Teachers College, Columbia University, in New York City.

Dr. Roger Erdvig is the headmaster at Wilmington Christian School in northern Delaware. With a doctorate in education from Liberty University, Roger also serves as an adjunct professor in the Church Leadership and Theology Department at the University of Valley Forge and speaks and consults on the topics of leadership, worldview development, and effective pedagogy.

Prologue

It had been a long week of conducting focus groups for a Christian school in the process of developing a new strategic plan. As is the case with such focus groups, the purpose was to ascertain what various stakeholders thought were the strengths and weaknesses of the school, its programs, and its people. The final focus group was to be conducted with a group of eight upper school students, mostly comprised of student leaders hand-picked by the high school principal. These would arguably be the most involved, enthusiastic, and (hopefully!) articulate students at the school.

As the students trickled into the conference room, I (Lynn) greeted them one by one and asked them to take a seat. We made small talk ("What grade are you in?" "How long have you been at the school?") until everyone had arrived. After I explained the purpose of the focus group and that their individual responses would be kept confidential, I launched into my list of questions about their experiences—what it was like being a student at the school, how responsive they felt the administration was to their concerns, what words they would use to describe the spiritual environment, how challenging and supportive were the teachers.

As I'd hoped, the group was talkative. I've found over the years that students—more so than any other group—have the most accurate pulse on school culture. This group didn't disappoint, and I quickly found out who the "best" teachers were, what current dress code controversy was raging (if hooded sweatshirts were allowed), and that chapel themes had become repetitive that school year.

There was just one problem I had in facilitating the group—a young man who had identified himself as the senior class president sat almost slumped over the table, looking down, and only answered questions with a mumbled "yes" or "no." I didn't have enough background to know if this was typical for him, or if he wasn't feeling well that day, or if he was suffering from a bad case of senioritis.

As the hour came to a close, and with most of my questions answered already, I decided to see if I could engage him. I knew the school had launched a service-learning program the year before and that his grade had been involved in an extensive veteran's project. Tied into their English and history courses, the project involved partnering with a local VFW hall to march in a Veteran's Day parade, visit some of the group's meetings, and host veterans in classes to discuss their experiences. The purpose of the project was both academic (for students to develop written and oral communication skills) as well as spiritual formation (cultivating empathy and care, and learning how to encourage others through practical service). The culminating event of the service-learning experience was a "Veteran's Night," when the students invited dozens of veterans to campus for a special student-served dinner, presentation of certificates of appreciation, and student-led musical performances. As a capstone to the entire year of service-learning, students interviewed veterans at their tables about their military service. Afterwards, students wrote essays about the veterans' stories for inclusion in a biography project, which was later shared with the veterans who had attended.

Armed with this information, I turned to the senior class president (who was still slumped over the table) and said, "So I know that you did a service-learning project with veterans last year. Can you tell me a little bit about it?"

While I was hoping to wake him up slightly, I wasn't prepared for what happened next—he sat bolt upright in his chair, banged his fist on the table, looked me straight in the eye, and loudly exclaimed, "I would do that again in a heartbeat!"

I was so startled that I barely managed to stammer a follow-up question—something along the lines of, "And why's that?"

We'll never forget his response—and it's the origin of our book title:

"Because," he replied, "*it brought it all to life.*"

We've pondered this student's words frequently in the years since. They have profound and multiple meanings. First, service-learning brought everything the student was *learning* in the classroom to life—meaning, rather than simply textbook knowledge about veterans, wartime literature, or how to write a biographical essay, his learning came alive through relationships with veterans and interacting with their stories. But service-learning was also powerful because it brought his learning to *life*—in other words, he could see how his knowledge about literature and history could be applied in practical ways outside of the classroom, to engage real people and to meet real needs. And, judging by his body language, service-learning brought *the student himself* to life— he found deep meaning and purpose in the Ephesians 2:10 work of service-learning: "*For we are his workmanship, created in Christ Jesus for good works, which God prepared beforehand, that we should walk in them.*"

While this is one student's story, it is representative of what we've seen repeated again and again at Christian schools implementing service-learning. When students connect classroom learning with genuine service to their communities, they not only master academic concepts better and learn how to apply them in real life, but also grow in their understanding of how God has uniquely fashioned them for His restoration work in the world. In this way, service-learning has the power to transform Christian education by truly "bringing it to life."

Introduction: Engaging Students through Service-Learning

In light of the unique needs of today's learners and the complex world for which schools are preparing them, Christian educators are searching for more effective ways to engage their students in the multifaceted learning, growth, and development articulated in their mission statements. To this end, service-learning is a powerful and promising pedagogy that has largely remained untapped in Christian schools. The purpose of this book is to provide a roadmap for Christian educators to harness the power of service-learning for transformation.

As we travel around the field of education in our different roles, we regularly hear from educators that today's students are markedly different from previous generations. There is a significant body of research that confirms this, and describes the unprecedented societal influences that are impacting students and the schools in which they are educated—such as all-encompassing and immersive technology, changes in family structures, diversity in learning abilities, and shifts in social and moral values (Twenge 2017). These and other influences have led to unique learning challenges for students, which in turn have translated into difficulty for educators in engaging their students in the learning process.

For these reasons, it has been our experience that educators are searching for teaching and learning strategies that more effectively facilitate student engagement. They are finding it is no longer sufficient to just transmit information to students; given students' access to unlimited information via the Internet, a traditional "chalk and talk" method of teaching is increasingly ineffective in engaging them. Moreover, from a research perspective, this kind of pedagogy has been shown to be insufficient for developing problem-solving, communication, and relational skills necessary for today's complex world (Colby et al. 2003, 133). Educators are discovering that just as today's students and the world itself have changed, so too must teaching and learning.

While we find this reality in almost every sector of education, it takes on unique meaning in Christian education. Christian schools are places where teachers and students engage the timeless truth of the Bible and its implications for the academic subjects under study. Christian schools are also communities in which spiritual formation and personal growth occur in the context of relationships. And Christian schools are situated within no less than three communities: of grace (both local expressions of the church and the enduring fellowship of believers in Christ); of a local geographical context (whether town, city, or country); and the global community (mediated by technology, and in which we are all interconnected).

Thus, at Christian schools we also hear another common theme: Christian educators are not content with students' "knowing all the right answers," but rather desire that students' hearts and minds be captured and transformed by knowing the God of truth, and that students would lead lives of faithfulness that extend His restorative work to their communities. As James K.A. Smith (2009) explains, "a Christian understanding of human persons should also shape how we teach, not just *what* we teach" (33, emphasis in original).

So how can Christian schools fulfill their essential missions while engaging today's students fully in their learning? How can we conceptualize teaching and learning in the Christian school in a way that has integrity with a biblical worldview, recognizes the authority of Scripture and the power of the Holy Spirit, and takes its direction from the Greatest Commandment and the Great Commission? Using Hunter's framing, what does "faithfully present" Christian education that is "adequate to the challenges of the present moment" (2010, 276–77) look like?

These are not easy questions, and likewise there are no easy answers. And unfortunately, the language we use in Christian education to formulate answers can be complex and elusive. Do we use the vocabulary of biblical worldview development, spiritual formation, integrating biblically, or teaching Christianly? Are we interested in engaged learning, deeper learning, student-centered learning, or transformative learning? Our answer to these and related questions is, simply, "yes!" This is our answer not only because resolving these philosophical and pedagogical tensions is beyond the scope of a practical guidebook, but also because we believe that the topic of this book can transcend these tensions. Regardless of our terminology, we think that harnessing the power of service—by integrating it thoroughly in teaching and learning in Christian schools—is a largely untapped way for Christian schools to enact their missions more fully in today's world.

This brings us to service-learning, which Colby et al. (2003) describe as "the most widespread and closely studied of the various student-centered, or engaged, pedagogies" (134).

Service-learning is a pedagogy that connects classroom learning with service opportunities in the community, in an iterative cycle where student learning is facilitated through structured reflection. There is significant evidence from research that service-learning has a positive impact on a range of student outcomes, including academic, social, and behavioral, and even students' views of the world and their role in it (we devote the first chapter of this book to defining and describing service-learning, as well as its outcomes). Our twenty years of collective experience and research with service-learning—with about half of that spent collaborating together in Christian school settings—confirms this. We have found service-learning to be a powerful approach for engaging students, maximizing their learning, nurturing their personal growth, developing their worldview, training them in serving others, and equipping them to "live out" Ephesians 2:10: "For we are his workmanship, created in Christ Jesus for good works, which God prepared beforehand, that we should walk in them."

As an approach to teaching and learning in the Christian school, service-learning requires intentionality, forethought, planning, and collaboration. This leads us to this book. In our work with schools we have received repeated requests for a "roadmap" for service-learning in the Christian school. In this book, we attempt to provide just that for both school leaders and teachers, by breaking down Christian service-learning into a set of tasks that have then been organized into chapters. These tasks include: defining service-learning (chapter 1); conceptually framing service-learning (chapter 2); guiding service-learning through standards (chapter 3); designing service-learning (chapter 4); supporting service-learning (chapter 5); and assessing service-learning (chapter 6). Finally, suggested resources for implementing service-learning are provided, along with worksheets and templates that we have used with success in Christian schools (chapter 7).

For each chapter, we provide case examples and vignettes to illustrate key concepts, which we have amassed in—and based off our work with—Christian schools. This is in response to our finding that most Christian educators have difficulty "visualizing" what service-learning looks like in action when first introduced to the concept. In our experience, providing concrete examples of service-learning projects helps to "jump start" educators' imagination for what service-learning might look like in their own contexts.

Finally, provided at the end of each chapter is a set of "next steps" as well as discussion questions. We strongly encourage you to engage in those questions with a team from your school. Because of its complex and intensive nature, service-learning works best when school leaders and teachers work collaboratively. Reading this book and answering the discussion questions as a group will not only set the groundwork for collaboration, but also foster the shared understanding and language necessary for service-learning to be successful.

As we will see in the first chapter, service-learning is a powerful means of involving students more in their learning. In turn, schools can ignite students' enthusiasm about using their God-given gifts to serve others and meet real needs, just as Jesus instructed and modeled for believers. Through this engagement, students have opportunity to learn the skills they will need for lifelong service, discover and develop their unique callings, and see their deeper purpose as part of God's redemptive story and plan. As fellow Christian educators, we pray that this book will help you harness the power of service-learning to those ends.

Next Steps

1. Find other educators at your school who share your interest in exploring service-learning, and form a book group to read through this book together. Utilize the discussion questions provided at the end of each chapter to guide your exploration.

2. Conduct an "audit" at your school of your students' opportunities to serve others. Once you identify these service opportunities, characterize them by type (e.g., community service requirement, one-time outreaches, ongoing campaigns or "drives," peer-to-peer service, mission trips, partnerships with local ministries, special courses, service-learning). This audit will be helpful to keep on hand as you read through this book and consider ways to strengthen service at your school.

Discussion Questions

1. What sparked your interest in this book?

2. What goals do you have for reading this book? In other words, what do you most want to get out of it?

3. How can you use this book to engage others in your school in a dialogue about service-learning?

1
Defining Service-Learning

Service-learning is a powerful pedagogy that connects classroom learning with service opportunities in the community, in an iterative cycle where student learning is facilitated through structured reflection. Although widespread in secular K–12 and postsecondary settings, service-learning is less commonly found in Christian schools. However, the outcomes of service-learning—such as positive gains in academic achievement, civic engagement, beliefs and values, and leadership, spiritual, and personal development—are closely aligned with Christian schools' missions, thereby suggesting the power of service-learning for Christian education.

Defining Service-Learning

At its essence, service-learning is a pedagogy that intentionally connects classroom learning with service opportunities outside of the school. Service-learning is one of several types of "experiential learning" methods, but it is unique in that "students engage in activities that address human and community needs together with structured opportunities intentionally designed to promote student learning and development" (Jacoby 1996, 5). Stanton, Giles, and Cruz (1999) point to the name "service-learning" as providing its definition, by joining "two complex concepts: community action, the 'service,' and efforts to learn from that action and connect what is learned to existing knowledge, the 'learning'" (2). Because of that connected relationship between service and learning, most authors hyphenate the term. Though it may be awkward (and some argue grammatically incorrect!) we agree that the "hyphen in service-learning is critical in that it symbolizes the symbiotic relationship between service and learning" (Jacoby 1996, 5).

In practice, we have seen service-learning happen in every grade level and anchored in nearly every subject. We've also seen a tremendous range of community sites for service-learning, including homeless shelters, literacy centers, nursing homes, Christian ministries, community gardens, health clinics, and local churches. With this wide range of grade levels, subjects, and locations for service, the possibilities for service-learning are limited only by the creativity of the faculty, students, and community partners involved.

Despite this diversity of what service-learning looks like in practice, all service-learning projects share common characteristics. We have identified four widely-accepted characteristics of service-learning through our work with schools, research on student outcomes, and reviews of the literature. Service-learning as a pedagogy:

1. Connects community service or outreach with classroom learning and the curriculum;
2. Takes students outside of the school setting and into the local community, to address real community needs;
3. Creates authentic, meaningful relationships between students and those being served; and
4. Increases and enhances student learning, as well as students' desire and ability to serve others.

Perhaps more importantly, we've heard much the same from students themselves. For example, in our qualitative focus groups and interviews with students over the years, they've told us that "what we learned in class came alive" through service-learning. Students have also said they "saw what it's really like in the community, and what we did there really made a difference." In terms of those they served, many students remarked that "we really got to know them, and they really appreciated what we did." Finally, when comparing service-learning experiences with more traditional learning, we've heard students literally exclaim, "I would do it again in a heartbeat!" All of these statements point to the impact that students themselves perceived regarding service-learning. This is remarkable because as educators, we often have to wait until years after students graduate for them to realize the value of their educational experiences. This is not the case with service-learning: the impact is almost always immediately recognized and valued by the learner.

In addition to these four characteristics, we've also found it useful to define service-learning by examining what it is *not*. There are four common educational activities that do not equate with service-learning, but that nonetheless are often confused with it. These are:

1. Community service or outreach with no linkage to the curriculum (including required community service hours, which are ubiquitous at Christian schools);

2. Service that does not take students into the community outside of the school (e.g., clean-up projects around the school grounds, or peer tutoring at the school);

3. Active learning without a direct service component, or that has no significant contact with those being served (such as creating a video, website, etc.); and

4. A one-time event, as opposed to sustained, multiple contacts with those being served (e.g., Christmas caroling at an assisted living facility).

All of these activities are certainly worthwhile, and we do not suggest that they are unimportant or inconsequential in the life of a Christian school or to students' experiences! However, we cannot link them through research to the same high degree of impact as we have seen with service-learning.

In addition to these four structural differences between service-learning and other types of learning experiences, there are two other differences to point out that are more philosophical in nature. First, from a pedagogical standpoint, it is critical to note that service-learning should not be an "add on" or "extra work," either for students or for teachers. Ideally, service-learning should be fully integrated into the curriculum. This means that service-learning should be planned, implemented, and assessed as intentionally as any other part of the academic program. In this way, service-learning can move toward the instructional "heart" of the school. Otherwise, service-learning not only remains peripheral to the mission of the school, but also creates challenges for faculty as they try to wedge service-learning into an already packed instructional plan.

Second, we want to point out that service-learning is not the same thing as charitable work, and that it operates from a community—not a charitable—perspective. Unlike charity, service-learning involves a true partnership between students and community members, as they work together to address a community need. It's easy to fall into the trap of an "us-versus-them" mentality, where community members are viewed as needy and the school is seen as coming to the rescue in some way.

This view is counterproductive for several reasons. It does not encourage students to develop humility in service, as Christ demonstrated when He washed the disciples' feet (John 13). Nor does it lead to authentic relationships, where community members feel valued as true partners. Further, a charity perspective can also be detrimental for school students who live in or come from the community in which the service is performed, as it sends mixed messages about their value and their community's value, and calls into question their sense of belonging at the school. Cumulatively, a charity perspective reinforces the separation between the Christian school and its surrounding community, as opposed to breaking down walls through genuine partnerships.

Some ways to ensure that a community (versus charity) perspective is used to frame service-learning at a Christian school include: providing a sound framework for serving (see chapter 2); selecting sites for service that are in close proximity to the school (which promotes sustained relationships and breaks down community-school barriers); and training teachers to be sensitive to the difference between a charity perspective and a community mindset, with the latter being more conducive to authentic service.

Service-Learning Case Story:
A Seventh Grade Class Uses Math to Address Hunger

A seventh-grade teacher chose to implement service-learning in conjunction with the math curriculum, targeting the specific units of percentages, proportional relationships, problem-solving and estimation, and consumer math. The teacher reasoned that linking math concepts to service-learning would not only help students to master these concepts but also enable them to learn how to serve others and solve real-world problems at the same time. The teacher went through the curriculum and swapped out existing examples and sample problems with ones that related to addressing the unmet food needs of the community. The teacher utilized the outcomes that had already been identified in the course's curriculum guide (relative to the specific math units being targeted), as well as drew upon the schoolwide expected student outcomes related to academic excellence, biblical servanthood, and personal growth in students' gifts and talents.

The teacher reached out to a local food pantry to partner in a service-learning project. The food pantry—which had a large distribution network throughout the surrounding towns and county—relied on donations from individuals and corporations to meet the significant community need for free groceries, due to a high unemployment rate. The seventh-grade class made four trips (one each academic quarter) to the food pantry, with the purpose of inventorying their supplies and identifying changes in supply and demand over the year. They returned to class, analyzed the data together, and created reports for the food pantry identifying trends.

In order to deepen and cement students' learning, the teacher required students to keep a biweekly journal in which they responded to structured reflection questions. These questions asked students to identify connections between their classroom learning and their service experiences, as well as reflect on how their work at the food pantry was helping them to grow in their unique gifts and talents, develop Christ-likeness, and help restore and repair brokenness in the world through service. These reflections were shared with two other students, who provided peer feedback, as well as with the teacher. The seventh-grade English teacher also worked with students in their English class to develop their journal responses and assisted the math teacher with grading the journals. Finally, the seventh-grade history teacher led reflective discussions on community hunger and its causes as a current event topic, and the students selected one of those causes on which to write a research paper. Working together, these three teachers—math, English, and history—coordinated their curriculum to support students' learning and reflection, even though the project officially was situated in their math class.

The Cycle of Service-Learning

We've defined service-learning as involving both classroom learning and service experiences in the community. While true, there is more to the story: service-learning is a complex pedagogy that resembles an iterative cycle as opposed to a linear process. In the cycle of service-learning, students modulate between classroom learning and service experiences, with reflection mediating learning between the two.

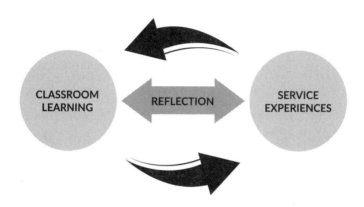

Classroom learning involves all of the course content and processes by which students engage that content (e.g., lessons, readings, assignments, and assessments). Ideally, service-learning is tied to course content throughout the academic year, rather than linked to a single unit or lesson. This not only expands the opportunity for student learning, but also serves to integrate service-learning more thoroughly in the curriculum. We do not mean to suggest that every class period is spent on topics related to service-learning; however,

> ***Service-Learning Snapshot:***
> *One sixth-grade science teacher decided to devote one class period out of every two weeks to the class' service-learning project, which involved serving in a community garden to promote healthy eating in their township. Class time was used for planning trips to work in the garden, reflection activities, and group discussions about project progress.*

the competencies and knowledge students will need in preparation for the service experiences themselves should be incorporated regularly throughout the course. Additionally, it is important to provide students with instruction on the biblical basis for service. (Such a framework, along with scriptural references that can be helpful to this end, is provided in chapter 2.)

Next, service experiences are opportunities for students to engage in meaningful service in the community outside of the school. Service experiences bear some similarities to field trips when it comes to logistics (insurance, permission slips, scheduling, transportation arrangements, budgeting for costs, etc.). However, service experiences differ significantly from field trips in terms of their purpose and format. The purpose of service experiences is to address real needs of the community partner, as defined by that partner. Needs to be addressed, as well as the ways to address them, are negotiated between the school and the service site. This partnership is what makes service-learning fundamentally different from charitable or philanthropic work (which tends to be unidirectional and non-relational). Thus, students in service-learning need to have ample opportunity to interact with those being served. This means that service-learning is also of sufficient duration and frequency for students to develop relationships with community partners. For these reasons, service experiences are in sharp contrast to the "one-off" approach for most field trips; rather, students should have a sense of personal investment in the work of, and with, the community partner. (Additional guidelines for best practices for service experiences are provided in chapter 3.)

Finally, *reflection* is an ongoing activity of thinking about and documenting personal experience and learning. Reflection is the pedagogical component of service-learning with which educators are often least familiar; nonetheless, it is critical. This is because reflection mediates—or provides the connective tissue—between classroom learning and service experiences. The power of reflection for learning is supported by research; for example, structured reflection in service-learning has been shown to be a primary predictor of positive academic outcomes (Eyler and Giles 1999). From a Christian perspective, reflection has been identified as a core means by which Christian young adults not only process their life experiences, but also build their understanding of the world through the lens of Scripture (Erdvig 2016).

Reflection is more than merely summarizing or reporting on accomplishments. Instead, it is "a vital and ongoing process in service-learning that integrates learning and experience with personal growth and awareness" (Kaye 2004, 11). As students consider their personal experience via structured reflection throughout the entire service-learning project, they are practicing higher-order thinking skills and learning to become more self-aware. Reflection can take many different forms, including journaling, guided discussion, creating artwork or poetry, and so forth. Bain et al. (2002) suggest that the specific format of reflection is not as important as the process, which can be seen as involving five steps:

1. *Reporting* involves simply documenting what happened or what was experienced, and includes a brief description of the trigger or prompt used to initiate the reflection;

2. *Responding* to the experience involves students' recording observations, feelings, and questions that arise;
3. *Relating* entails making connections between the experience and students' other experiences, skills, knowledge, and understanding;
4. *Reasoning* involves students' explaining the meaning of the experience, and they can be encouraged to answer the question "so what?" to help explain meaning; and
5. *Reconstructing* is the final phase, in which students draw new conclusions and develop plans for how to interact with similar experiences in the future, and students make a commitment to change and incorporate new learnings into their perspectives.

Reflection opportunities should be structured in such a way as to move students in an age-appropriate and developmentally consistent manner through this progression, toward higher levels of integrating their learning from classroom and service experiences.

Because of the importance of reflection to service-learning, faculty should intentionally incorporate reflection activities into lesson planning for service-learning. Put simply, reflection opportunities can't be left to chance any more than a trip to a service site can be unplanned. (More specific guidance for planning, along with a template that incorporates reflection as a key component of service-learning, is provided in chapter 4.)

The Power of Service-Learning

With service-learning now defined, we turn to mapping the power of service-learning for the Christian school setting— which we contend has not yet been fully realized. To this end, it's helpful to begin with an understanding of how service-learning developed in educational practice.

Service-learning as a specific pedagogy first emerged on the U.S. education scene in the 1960s and has grown in popularity since. The term *service-learning* first appeared in 1964, in conjunction with service programs at the Oak Ridge Associated Universities in Tennessee (White 2001). Undergraduate service-learning programs flourished over the next few decades in colleges and universities across the United States. As service-learning's popularity grew in individual universities, various associations and councils were formed to encourage service-learning and to provide for research of its impact and best practices, such as The Project for Public and Community Service, The National Center for Service-Learning for Early Adolescents, and The Learn and Serve America National Service-Learning Clearinghouse.

The 1980s were marked by increased government funding for the development of service-learning programs, culminating in 1993 with the renewal of the National and Community Service Act. Service-learning has continued to grow since that time, to where an estimated 24% of colleges and universities now include service-learning in their programs, as do 35% of public high schools, 25% of public middle schools, and 20% of public elementary schools (Kielsmeier 2011).

By way of contrast, service-learning has not gained

the same popularity in Christian schools, though most Christian schools do offer extracurricular community service or outreach experiences. The lack of service-learning experiences in Christian schools is puzzling, as the research on service-learning (discussed in detail below) suggests that it leads to several valuable outcomes. Beyond greater mastery of content and course-specific learning goals, service-learning has also been shown to elicit multidimensional change in students, including positive impact on overall academic achievement, commitment to civic engagement, formation of beliefs and values, growth in leadership competencies and personal development, and a lasting commitment to serving others. This list bears a striking resemblance to the vision and mission statements of many Christian schools.

The research findings on service-learning tend to fall into four broad categories: (1) academic achievement; (2) civic engagement; (3) beliefs and values; and (4) leadership, spiritual, and personal development.

1. Academic Achievement

There is reasonably strong evidence in the literature that service-learning has a positive effect on many aspects of student learning. At the college level, participation has been associated with higher course grades and student reporting of higher levels of satisfaction with their learning experiences (Berson and Younkin 1998), as well as higher GPA, greater retention, a greater likelihood of degree completion, more interaction with faculty, and gains in academic knowledge (Astin, Sax, and Avalos 1999). A positive correlation has also been found between service-learning and improved writing skills (Vogelgesang and Astin 2000) as well as deeper learning of classroom content (Felten and Clayton 2011).

Research at the K–12 level has identified similar outcomes of service-learning. For example, a meta-analysis of research on service-learning concluded that service-learning contributes to gains in student achievement (Warren 2012). Research has also show that service-learning participants at both the elementary and secondary levels outperform students on the ELA sections of achievement tests, regardless of which classes included a service-learning component (Furco and Root 2010).

2. Civic Engagement

Service-learning has been shown to contribute to the development of civic values, knowledge, skills, efficacy, and commitment (Eyler and Giles 1999). Moreover, students engaged in course-based service-learning have been found to experience significant gains in their civic behavior and concern for civic responsibility, while students involved in either extracurricular community service or no service activities showed no growth or even declined in those domains (Myers-Lipton 1998). When a broader definition of civic engagement as "involvement in the public life of a community" (Prentice 2007, 136) is used—to include political and nonpolitical organizations, as well as charitable work initiatives—research suggests that service-learning fosters a disposition toward wide and varied community involvement (Prentice 2007; cf. Colby et al. 2003).

3. Beliefs and Values

Involvement in service-learning has been shown to foster

the development of students' beliefs and values (Radecke 2007). This is of particular interest for Christian schools, which are missionally committed to shaping the values of their students. In terms of values, the research suggests that positive and constructive attitudes toward learning and school in general are a consistent outcome of participation in service-learning (Furco and Root 2010). This could be a result of the highly engaging nature of service-learning, as students tend to have positive attitudes about learning in which they are actively involved and in which they are interested (Colby et al. 2003). These two characteristics—active involvement and engaging students' interest—are hallmarks of service-learning (Rama et al. 2000).

4. Leadership, Spiritual, and Personal Development
Service-learning inherently involves students in collaborating with one another and with adult mentors to generate solutions to community problems. This collaboration provides practice in navigating group dynamics including leadership, negotiation, and communication, and the literature suggests that service-learning is correlated with gains in these areas (Furco and Root 2010; Carver 1997). Service-learning has also been shown to enhance other domains of development, including self-efficacy, agency, identity formation, sense of well-being, and career planning (Felten and Clayton 2011).

Participation in service-learning has also led to students reporting "greater self-knowledge, spiritual growth, and finding reward in helping others" as well as served as a predictor of "an increased sense of personal efficacy," "desire to include service to others in one's career plans," and students feeling connected to the community and having a stronger relationship with faculty and peers (Eyler and Giles 1999, 55). While faith formation is a multi-faceted and complex process that occurs over time (Fowler 2000), service-learning may be a promising pedagogy to foster this development. In terms of community and career involvement, service-learning participation has also been correlated with both additional volunteer work and choosing careers in the helping or serving professions (Vogelsang and Astin 2000).

While this research was not conducted in Christian schools, there is still much encouragement from these findings. Namely, if service-learning can impact students in secular settings—where participation is correlated with positive gains in academic achievement, community engagement, beliefs and values, and leadership, spiritual, and personal development—it isn't hard to imagine the impact that service-learning might have in Christian schools, where these outcomes are closely tied to schools' mission.

Next Steps

1. Review the audit of service opportunities that you generated at the end of the introduction. Assess how many of those opportunities fit the definition of service-learning as provided in this chapter.

2. Obtain your school's expected student outcomes (ESOs). If your school does not have ESOs, you likely have a "profile of a graduate," broad course targets, or another list that enumerates the intended student learning outcomes of your school or individual course. Review the research on the outcomes of service-learning provided in this chapter, and circle

on your list any places of overlap (where the known outcomes of service-learning connect with the desired outcomes of your school or course).

Discussion Questions

1. Think about your understanding of service-learning prior to reading this chapter. Has it changed in any way, and if so, how?

2. When looking at the cycle of service-learning, which component—classroom learning, service experiences, or reflection—do you think will be the most challenging to envision and enact in your own setting?

3. Reflect on any overlap between the known outcomes of service-learning (academic achievement, civic engagement, beliefs and values, and leadership, spiritual, and personal development) and the expected student outcomes of your school or course. If the overlap is significant, how might service-learning be a promising practice for your school?

2
Framing Service-Learning

In this chapter we lay out a framework for service-learning in Christian education, composed of four key concepts: Christ-likeness; Responsive Service; Worldview Development; and God's Eternal Purpose. After describing each in detail, the chapter concludes by discussing how this distinctly Christian model of service-learning is well-suited to the mission of the Christian school.

Having described service-learning as a pedagogy in the preceding chapter, we turn to the question of what it means to engage in service-learning in the Christian school. John Hull (2003) identifies "Christian perspective as the defining concept in Christian education" (206), or that which fundamentally makes Christian education distinctive from other forms of schooling. Although there may be similarities between how service-learning looks in Christian schools versus other settings, the question this chapter seeks to answer is how that Christian perspective informs and shapes a *uniquely Christian* approach to service-learning. As Hull goes on to explain, "Christian perspective must reshape and redirect the curriculum, pedagogical theory, student evaluation, educational goals, and school structure" (207). There is no part of the educational process that is untouched or uninformed by a Christian perspective—and this ought to hold true for service-learning as well.

In our work with schools, we have proposed using four key concepts to establish a distinctively Christian perspective of service-learning: 1. *Christ-likeness*; 2. *Responsive Service*; 3. *Worldview Development*; and 4. *God's Eternal Purpose*. The illustration below provides a visual of this framework.

While we discuss each side of the framework in further detail below, we want to first mention the benefits we have seen when Christian educators use this framework. First and foremost, it helps schools to ground the practice of service-learning in Scripture. It also provides schools with a common language that ties their mission to service-learning. And finally, the framework can inform the planning of service-learning projects, faculty professional development for service-learning, and direct instruction to students about the purpose and goals of service-learning.

Christ-likeness

At the top of our frame for Christian service-learning is *Christ-likeness*, in recognition of Christ's preeminence as "... the head of the body, the church. He is the beginning, the firstborn from the dead, that in everything he might be preeminent" (Colossians 1:18). By placing this concept at the top, we are acknowledging that Christ is our goal as well as our model in all things (Matthew 10:25). Through service-learning that nurtures their development of Christ-likeness, students serve as He served—including leading by serving others.

To explore the concept of Christ-likeness, we turn to the

account in the Gospel of John, chapter 13, of Jesus washing His disciples' feet at the Last Supper. In this familiar passage, Jesus addresses a very practical need of the time and location (dirt roads + sandals = dirty feet). Over Peter's protests and then hesitant acquiescence, Jesus finishes the demeaning task and then seizes the opportunity to teach His disciples: "If I then, your Lord and Teacher, have washed your feet, you also ought to wash one another's feet. For I have given you an example, that you should do as I have done to you" (John 13: 14–15, NKJV). While the image of foot washing doesn't have much coinage in today's society (thanks to paved roads and Payless!), there are many ways to meet practical needs in modern times. Jesus makes it clear that we should follow His example in doing so, with genuine humility. Thus, in this first principle, we serve because He first served; in doing so, we become more like Him and grow in Christ-likeness.

We also learn from Scripture that Jesus defines true leadership as serving others. We see this specifically in the account in the Gospel of Mark chapter 10, when Jesus responds to the request of James and John to sit on either side of Him in His glory. When the other ten disciples become angry at the brothers' power play, Jesus responds by contrasting how worldly rulers act with how His disciples should act. While the former "lord it over" others (Mark 10:42, NKJV), Jesus explains that for His disciples, "Whoever desires to become great among you shall be your servant" as "even the Son of Man did not come to be served, but to serve, and to give His life a ransom for many" (vss. 43-45). While the concept of servant leadership is found in secular organizational and leadership theories, it is clearly biblical.

In addition to these accounts from the Gospels, we find the following Scriptures that point us toward Christ-likeness in service:

Acts 20:35	In all things I have shown you that by working hard in this way we must help the weak and remember the words of theLord Jesus, how he himself said, 'It is more blessed to give than to receive.'
1 Corinthians 11:1	Be imitators of me, as I am of Christ.
Ephesians 5:1–2	Therefore be imitators of God, as beloved children. And walk in love, just as Christ also loved us and gave Himself up for us, a fragrant offering and sacrifice to God.
Philippians 2:5–11	Have this mind among yourselves, which is yours in Christ Jesus, who, though he was in the form of God, did not count equality with God a thing to be grasped, but emptied himself, by taking the form of a servant, being born in the likeness of men. And being found in human form, he humbled himself by becoming obedient to the point of death, even death on a cross Therefore God has highly exalted him and bestowed on him the name that is above every name, so that at the name of Jesus every knee should bow, in heaven and on earth and under the earth, and every tongue confess that Jesus Christ is Lord, to the glory of God the Father.
1 John 2:6	Whoever says he abides in him ought to walk in the same way in which he walked.

In these texts, we find that Jesus is our example that we are to follow in serving others, including when we are leading. We become more like Him as we follow Him; thus, service-learning offers students a powerful opportunity to grow as His disciples who bear Christ's image.

Responsive Service

Directly below Christ-likeness, and at the bottom of the frame, is *Responsive Service*. Just as we know that we love because He first loved us (1 John 4:19), when we serve it is in response to who Jesus is and what He has already done for us through His life, death, and resurrection. It is thus our joy to be counted friends of our Lord—the opposite of slavish duty—as we are obedient to His call to serve: "You are my friends if you do what I command you" (John 15:14). Service-learning is an opportunity for our students to respond to the Person, goodness, and work of Jesus by loving others. As 1 John 3:16 explains, "By this we know love, that he laid down his life for us, and we ought to lay down our lives for the brothers."

Viewed from this perspective, it is not an accident that Jesus equates serving others with serving Him. In the Matthew 25 parable of the sheep and the goats, the sheep—or the ones who inherit the kingdom of God—will be those who engaged in practical acts of service: they fed the hungry; provided water to the thirsty; took in strangers; clothed the naked; and visited the sick and imprisoned. But it's clear from this parable that Jesus takes these acts personally: "And the King will answer them, 'Truly, I say to you, as you did it to one of the least of these my brothers, you did it to me.'" (Matthew 25:40). We see in these Scriptures that any act of service we perform is ultimately a responsive service to Jesus, the One with whom we are in relationship that He Himself initiated. Additionally, we know we are saved by grace through faith in Christ (Ephesians 2:8–9), but Scripture views that faith as being borne out in our actions. As 1 John 3:18 encourages us, "Little children, let us not love in word or talk but in deed and in truth," and James 2:14–18 culminates with the statement, "Show me your faith apart from your works, and I will show you my faith by my works." Our salvation by grace leads us to respond by loving and serving others. We see this theme echoed throughout Scripture:

1 Corinthians 9:19	For though I am free from all, I have made myself a servant to all, that I might win more of them.
Galatians 5:13–14	For you were called to freedom, brothers. Only do not use your freedom as an opportunity for the flesh, but through love serve one another. For the whole law is fulfilled in one word: "You shall love your neighbor as yourself."
Galatians 6:2	Bear one another's burdens, and so fulfill the law of Christ.
Ephesians 2:10	For we are his workmanship, created in Christ Jesus for good works, which God prepared beforehand, that we should walk in them.
Philippians 2:1–4	So if there is any encouragement in Christ, any comfort from love, any participation in the Spirit, any affection and sympathy, complete my joy by being of the same mind, having the same love, being in full accord and of one mind. Do nothing from selfish ambition or conceit, but in humility count others more significant than yourselves. Let each of you look not only to his own interests, but also to the interests of others.

Titus 3:14	And let our people learn to devote themselves to good works, so as to help cases of urgent need, and not be unfruitful.
Hebrews 10:24	And let us consider how to stir up one another to love and good works.
Hebrews 13:1–3	Let brotherly love continue. Do not neglect to show hospitality to strangers, for thereby some have entertained angels unawares. Remember those who are in prison, as though in prison with them, and those who are mistreated, since you also are in the body.
Hebrews 13:16	Do not neglect to do good and to share what you have, for such sacrifices are pleasing to God.

From these Scriptures, we infer that service-learning offers students a powerful opportunity to respond to the saving work God has done in their lives, and by doing so deepen their relationship with Him. Even for those students who have not yet come to faith, they can be guided toward a deeper appreciation of salvation and its outworking in the life of a believer through responsive service.

Worldview Development

On the left side of the frame is the concept of Worldview Development, which we place on a longer side because this concept provides a "long view" of human development. A worldview is a meaning-making system that not only guides people's knowing and reasoning, but also shapes their responses to the world and the ways they act in it. As a powerful pedagogy, service-learning provides opportunity for students to continue to develop their worldview—and for teachers to shape that development in the direction of learning and applying biblical truth by serving others. Worldviews comprise a set of foundational assumptions concerning reality, including a sense of self and one's place in the world and convictions about what is true, valuable, and good (Koltko-Rivera 2004; Pearcy 2004; Sire 1997). Multiple authors have suggested lists of questions that a worldview answers, including: Where did everything come from? Is there a God? What is the nature of ultimate reality? What is the meaning of life? What is our purpose? Is there right and wrong? Why does it seem that the world is not as is should be? What happens after we die? Where is history going? What is a human being? Who am I? (Phillips, Brown, and Stonestreet 2008, 9). The answers to these questions compose a set of presuppositions that guide all of an individual's thinking and perceptions. In turn, a worldview provides a basis for behavior; individuals act according to their worldview, whether they do so intentionally or not (Valk 2013).

An important question for Christian educators is what, exactly, makes a worldview *biblical*. At the cognitive level, a worldview that is biblical involves a "framework of assumptions about reality, all of which are in submission to Christ" (Schultz and Swezey 2013, 232). This includes truths about the existence of God and who He reveals himself to be in creation, the Bible, and the person of Jesus Christ (Phillips, Brown, and Stonestreet 2008).

A biblical worldview goes beyond cognition, however. Sire (2015) posits that this worldview encompasses "heart orientation"—or a posture of worship toward God as the ultimate reality. And, as already noted, a biblical worldview "is actualized in our behavior" (Sire 2015, 153). We can see this readily in Scripture; the book of James (1:22–25; 2:14–26) repeatedly calls Christians to action, and Jesus Himself rebuked the religious leaders of His day for knowing the law but failing to live it out (Matthew 23). Clearly, having the right answers to life's big questions neatly filed away in one's head is insufficient. A biblical worldview must go beyond learning the correct answers to living that worldview out in one's daily decisions and commitments. In fact, Steven Garber (2007) suggest that the degree of alignment of behavior with heart orientation and rationally held presuppositions is a significant aspect of a maturing worldview. In other words, the whole of a biblical worldview is greater than the sum of its parts.

Christian educators are particularly interested in how a worldview is formed, as it is one of the central purposes of Christian schooling (Schultz and Swezey 2013). Sire (2015) suggests that a person's worldview is shaped and formed throughout the entire course of life, mediated by experience and social context. Erdvig (2016) found that in addition to Sire's dimensions (heart orientation, cognitive propositions, and behavioral alignment), biblical worldview development in emerging adulthood also involved three worldview "dispositions": awareness of one's worldview; ownership of the process of worldview development; and a commitment to meaningful processing (i.e., reflection).

All of these elements—experience, social context, self-awareness, ownership, and reflection—are hallmarks of service-learning. Through service-learning, Christian school students are challenged to move beyond "book learning" to apply their learning to real-world challenges and needs through serving others. Service-learning provides students with the opportunity to "live out" their developing worldviews and apply them through the action of service.

Interestingly, the research on service-learning outcomes in secular settings confirms its potential for shaping worldview development. As discussed in chapter 1, participation in service-learning is correlated with positive gains in beliefs and values, community engagement, and leadership, spiritual, and personal development. Many of these outcomes could be considered "markers" for worldview development. If these kinds of outcomes—which again may be reflective of overall worldview change—are seen in secular settings, it isn't hard to imagine the potential of service-learning for impacting worldview development in Christian schools.

God's Eternal Purpose

Finally, on the right side of the frame for service-learning is *God's Eternal Purpose*, which again is placed there because of its "long view"—but this time, the view is of human history, and every individual and institution's place in it. All people and the institutions we populate (including Christian schools) are all situated in God's great and enduring story of creation, fall, redemption, and restoration, as told through the metanarrative arc of the Bible. Garber (2014) draws upon Augustine to explain:

> [H]uman beings are story-shaped people, stretched between what ought to be and what will be. In our imaginings, our longings, at our best and at our worst, we are people whose identities are formed by a narrative that begins at the beginning and ends at the ending—the story of Scripture itself, of creation, fall, redemption and consummation.... It is a long story, and a complex story, and it is our story (202).

Service-learning enables students—as God's image-bearers, who are uniquely fashioned—to play a part in bringing God's redemptive work to the world, which manifests His presence and makes known His eternal purpose for humanity. The same can be said of the Christian school, as service-learning can become a vehicle for schools to purposefully engage in restoration work in their communities.

We can explain this better by starting back at the beginning, when God created Adam and Eve in His image (Genesis 1:26–27). As God's image-bearers, people were created to be "very good," with abilities (or gifts and talents) that were to be used to cultivate and steward creation. As Donovan Graham (2009) explains, "The calling and task of humankind as originally decreed by God has never changed" (103). People today are still engaged in creating, cultivating, developing, growing, and learning, even if the object of their activity is not relationship with and worship of the Creator. The Christian school's role is to recognize that students are created in God's image with these abilities, and that each is uniquely designed for the life described in Ephesians 2:10 (ESV): "For we are his workmanship, created in Christ Jesus for good works, which God prepared beforehand, that we should walk in them." Service-learning gives students real opportunities to develop their skills and abilities (academic, relational, vocational, and so forth) and to engage productively in God's appointed good works.

In the biblical narrative, we next take a sharp turn from creation to the fall of humanity, through the disobedience of Adam and Eve that brought sin and death into the world. The fall is the reason there is widespread suffering, pain, and need in the world. Service-learning enables Christian school students to see this brokenness in the world firsthand. Certainly they can see it many other places (often in their homes, neighborhoods, on the news, and in their own hearts), but the beauty of service-learning is that the educative power of the Christian school is brought to bear on students' view of fallen reality, through direct exposure and reflection— mediated by Christian teachers who can serve as mentors and guides in the process.

Service-learning offers the chance for students to not only recognize and understand the brokenness they encounter in the world, but also to realize that the only solution is the redemptive work of God. In the biblical narrative, we recognize Jesus was the only one who could help us in our broken state. It was entirely because of God's initiation through the Incarnation, and His work on the cross, that we have access again to God and to true life. Graham (2009) provides a powerful picture of God's redemptive work and its implications for the lives we are to live as believers:

> God did not sit back and say "how awful, but that is just the way it is." Neither can those who seek to reflect who He is ... We can readily see that our calling will not allow us simply to be content with souls that are saved and personal behavior that is ethical. God Himself identified with His people and came to them to live in their presence. The incarnation is a marvelous lesson in how we are meant to live out the image of God in the current age (105).

This reminds us of responsive service, as discussed earlier: our service is in response to God's work of grace, "so that no one can boast" (Ephesians 2:9). Likewise, "we have this treasure in jars of clay, to show that the surpassing power belongs to God and not to us" (2 Corinthians 4:7).

Graham's (2009) work is once again insightful regarding restoration, which he states is "perhaps most relevant for the teacher, those who are redeemed will act in that creation and toward others in ways that bring healing and restoration—a tangible demonstration of God's character" (102). He outlines several ways that "our behavior as redeemed image-bearers should make a difference in the culture" (104) including:

- Bringing *healing* by addressing "the economic conditions that produce suffering [and] the social conditions that produce isolation and loneliness" (104);
- Being agents of *renewal* by "taking something that already exists and making something better of it … [like] renewal in our cities, housing projects, corrupt governments, and industry that has so little concern for its workers … We are called to build something better that reflects the glory of God in its completion and operation just as the new heaven and new earth will" (104);
- Working for *deliverance* of others, as "redemptive activity should remove us and others from the bondage prevailing in the kingdom of darkness … poverty, drugs, sexual immorality, racial oppression. Image-bearing activity will lead us to attempt (through God's power) to break the rule that such things have over the lives of people in our world" (105);
- Advocating for *justice*, to "right those wrongs precipitated by the fall, especially those we inflict on one another" (105) wherever we may find them, whether in the legal system, unethical business practice, or elsewhere; and

- Seeking God's peace, or shalom, that "reflects the wholeness and togetherness God intended," whether in caring for the environment as part of God's creation or caring for others around us (105).

The power of service-learning for the Christian school lies in its capacity to engage students in all of these restoration activities. Ultimately, service-learning can orient students toward a lifetime of restorative work on behalf of our God who is Creator, Savior, Sustainer, and Redeemer, by teaching them to be ambassadors of Christ, who can make a difference in the fallen state of their communities and neighborhoods. Through this process, students can come to see their true purpose in God's story, and how they have been uniquely created and gifted by Him as active participants in that story.

Service-Learning Snapshot: A comprehensive service-learning program at a Christian high school involved students in a number of yearlong service opportunities, including projects that helped to provide social interaction to seniors in a nursing home, worked to address human trafficking by partnering with a local parachurch ministry, promoted racial reconciliation through helping to organize community dialogues, sponsored literacy and sports outreach programs aimed at helping to keep juveniles out of the criminal justice system, and engaged in conservation efforts at a local waterway. For each experience—which was linked to key units in the curriculum at every grade level—teachers explicitly connected the students' service with God's eternal purpose and the restorative work in which the students were engaged. Through structured journals and self-assessments, teachers also helped the students to reflect on how God had uniquely equipped each of them to contribute to that work. One chapel service per month was dedicated to service-learning, in which students had opportunities to share stories and pictures from their service experiences, as well as invite partner organizations to share about their work. This helped students to see themselves and their school as active participants in God's larger story of creation, fall, redemption, and restoration.

Putting It All Together

Like a picture frame, the four sides of our framework for service-learning are meant to work together. Not only do they complement each other, but also there is significant overlap and points of connection between them all. Ultimately, we believe this framework is sufficient for "holding up" the unique portraits of service-learning that Christian schools will paint. But we recognize that service-learning is not a silver bullet—powerful, yes, but by no means a panacea. We agree with Garber (2014) when he writes in *Visions of Vocation: Common Grace for the Common Good*:

> There is no more difficult task, holding one's individual and institutional responsibility for the way the world turns out—knowing the worst of the human heart and the corporate embodiment of that heart and still choosing to be responsible, for love's sake. But that task is ours. In our social and political situations, in our families and neighborhoods ... in this terribly complex world, full of wonder and wounds as it is (224).

We encourage you to reread this passage but add the words "Christian schools" after "families and neighborhoods"! When you do, it's clear that service-learning provides a powerful way for the Christian school to take "responsibility," as Garber describes it. Service-learning won't solve all of the problems that accompany this fallen world, either in our communities or in our students. But taking responsibility is what God requires of us, as, "He has told you, O man, what is good; and what does the Lord require of you but to do justice, and to love kindness, and to walk humbly with your God?" (Micah 6:8).

Similarly, we appreciate the way John Hambrick (2016) uses the phrase "move toward the mess" to describe "when folks get serious about engaging with the messy situations that exist across the street, across town, or across the world" (9). Moving toward the mess means "getting close enough for people to notice" (17) and to "engage with the brokenness of the world" (35). Service-learning provides Christian schools with a means of moving toward the mess in their communities and in the world writ large, and in doing so teach students to do the same throughout their lives—all while developing their identities, worldview, and God-given talents. It's a powerful and promising way for Christian schools to paint a portrait of Jesus through service, even if that portrait is like seeing "in a mirror dimly" (1 Corinthians 13:12). His amazing grace and divine power ensures that even the dim picture we paint of God is powerful enough for His restoration work.

Distinctly Christian Service-Learning

Although we hope we have presented a compelling framework for Christian service-learning, we recognize that there are competing frames that are offered in secular literature and practice. As discussed earlier, service-learning is a well-established pedagogy in much of public K–12 education, while Christian education has lagged behind. While we speculate that there are multiple reasons for this, there are two concerns that we want to address here: first, the question of whether service-learning is simply an education "fad"; and second, whether service-learning philosophically fits with the distinctive mission of Christian schools.

Anyone involved with education has seen a number of teaching methods come and go with frequency. The wavering between phonics-based and whole-language instruction in teaching reading is a micro-level example, and national educational standards and initiatives—including the Common Core—are macro-level examples. However, the fact that service-learning participation, scholarship, and funding remain strong after four decades of widespread engagement at many educational levels across the country indicates that it is here to stay. This staying power of service-learning is likely due to the empirical evidence for its multiple benefits for student outcomes, as research has already shown that service-learning is highly effective in impacting multiple domains of human development and across subject areas (Swaner and Brownell 2008). In addition, there are diverse formulations of service-learning, which means there isn't a "one-size-fits-all" prescription. We have therefore seen that service-learning "works" and that it can be adapted to fit different kinds of settings. Because of the importance of serving others to the Christian faith, and therefore to the Christian school, we believe that service-learning is all the more suited to Christian education.

Secondly, we wish to address the wariness we sometimes encounter among Christian educators toward educational methods that they perceive as originating from secular philosophies. We know this is a genuine concern, because we have heard teachers and administrators object to using service-learning or other active learning methods because they feature prominently in constructivist models of education. These educators argue that because the philosophical aims of these secular models are often at odds with a Christian worldview, the methodologies they employ must also be antithetical to Christian education.

Our response to such concerns is that, as we have shown in our framework for service-learning, the importance of serving others is a pervasive principle in Scripture. This is supported by the example of Jesus' own teaching, as He used a variety of methods to instruct His disciples. These include:

- Direct teaching on serving (itself diverse, involving didactic instruction and parables);
- Questioning (e.g., in Luke 10:36, when Jesus asks an expert in the law to reflect on the story of the good Samaritan: "Which of these three, do you think, proved to be a neighbor to the man who fell among the robbers?");
- Modeling (washing His disciples' feet, as discussed earlier);
- Guided practice (such as the feeding of the 5,000 in Luke 9:12–17); and
- Unsupervised practice (sending out of the disciples out to serve others in Luke 9:1–6, 10).

Jesus, who "knew all people" (John 2:24), understood that people learn in varied ways and need practical opportunities to apply their learning. Further, we can say confidently that Jesus taught and practiced these approaches well before modern-day educational philosophers realized their power for learning.

On a practical level, we encourage educators who are interested in service-learning to seek out useful resources to help them in thinking about designing projects (see chapter 7, where we list several), but of course recognize where those sources may diverge from a Christian worldview. Secular service-learning has much to offer Christian educators, particularly in the area of identifying best practices and deriving standards from those practices. When looking at materials to adopt for service-learning, though, it is important to do so thoughtfully and to review sources for their philosophical orientation and biases. This is no different, however, from any other educational practice or concept that a Christian educator might research or try out! Even here, God is the one who gives us wisdom in all things (Ecclesiastes 2:26, Colossians 2:2–3, James 3:17, James 1:5).

Finally, while many national service-learning organizations, consortia, and foundations are welcoming to nonpublic schools, there are few if any groups of Christian schools that collaborate in the area of service-learning. As Christian schools work to incorporate or expand service-learning, it's important to be mindful of ways to share successes with the broader community of Christian educators. Christian schools can formally or informally partner with other schools engaged in service-learning for the purpose of sharing strategies and learning from each other's efforts—and ultimately, building a larger body of scholarship and practice base for service-learning that is distinctly Christian.

Next Steps

Review your school's mission statement and the school or course list of expected student outcomes (ESOs). (If your school does not have ESOs, you may have a "profile of a graduate," broad course targets, or another list that enumerates the intended student learning outcomes of your school or course.) Using the framework for service-learning provided in this chapter, list any overlap or connections between your mission statement and ESOs and each side of the framework. For example, if the school's mission statement includes development of students' worldview as one of the school's goals, note that in the "Points of Connection" box on the left side.

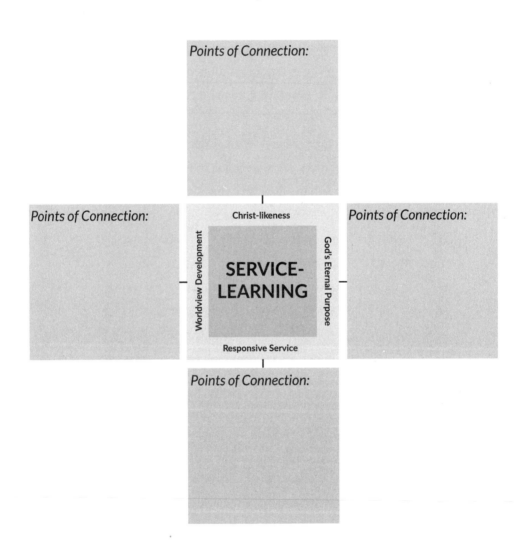

Points of Connection:

Points of Connection:

Points of Connection:

Christ-likeness

Worldview Development

SERVICE-LEARNING

God's Eternal Purpose

Responsive Service

Points of Connection:

Discussion Questions

1. Do the four sides of the service-learning framework—Christ-likeness, Responsive Service, Worldview Development, and God's Eternal Purpose—resonate with our vision of teaching and learning at our school? How or how not?

2. At our school, do faculty intentionally teach like Jesus did—using multiple methods, and engaging learners in the learning process? How so? And how can they do so even more?

3. How should service-learning at our school look and feel different from service-learning at the public school down the road?

3
Guiding Service-Learning

It has been said that there are as many formulations of service-learning in practice as there are service-learning projects. Given this diversity, it is important for schools to become familiar with guidelines that promote effective service-learning practice. This chapter presents a set of national standards for K–12 service-learning, along with supplemental standards for Christian schools, which can be used to guide planning and evaluating service-learning.

Why Consider Standards?

Standards have proliferated in K–12 education for many years, sometimes to the point of fatiguing educators. In light of this, it's helpful to review why standards are important and how they can be useful for planning, implementing, and evaluating service-learning. When standards reflect research on best practices, they help identify the key aspects or characteristics of practice that lend themselves to effectiveness, regardless of the specific project or school setting. This is important because although they may share similarities, no two service-learning projects are exactly alike—just as no two Christian schools are exactly alike. So, while looking to examples of service-learning projects is helpful for generating project ideas (and we offer a few such examples throughout this book), standards are important in that they provide guidelines for good practice across projects and settings.

It's particularly beneficial to examine standards early on in considering service-learning as a pedagogy for one's classroom or school (which is why this chapter precedes chapter 4, which deals with project planning). Developing service-learning projects requires creativity, imagination, and innovation, and we have seen in practice that it is easy to become "carried away" with an idea for a project without stopping to make sure it reflects best practices—and that it is truly service-learning.

By way of example, we worked with one high school math teacher who became excited about service-learning and wanted students to explore the lack of basic financial literacy among teenagers (and become financially literate themselves in the process). While this was a great problem to address, the teacher's solution was for students to develop a series of videos on financial topics that they would post online, like how to read a paycheck and understand payroll deductions. We had to help the teacher to see that while this was a great project that engaged students in active learning, it was not service-learning: there were no community partners involved, and consequently students had no direct and sustained contact with anyone outside of their class. (Ultimately, the teacher's principal encouraged the teacher to pursue the project, as both the teacher and the students were passionate about the idea, and it made for a great hands-on learning experience. However, it was not service-learning).

In this example, we found that referring to standards for service-learning helped provide clarity for both the teacher and the school principal. Thus, we would suggest that schools interested in pursuing service-learning take time to review standards together as team to help shape expectations for how to develop projects. In this chapter we present two sets of standards that we have used with schools to this end. The first set is the K–12 Service-Learning

Standards for Quality Practice (National Youth Leadership Council 2008). These research-based standards, which are widely used across K–12 settings, address eight core areas: (1) meaningful service; (2) link to curriculum; (3) reflection; (4) diversity; (5) youth voice; (6) partnerships; (7) progress monitoring; and (8) duration and intensity.

In addition to the NYLC standards, we have developed a second set of standards, the K–12 Supplemental Service-Learning Standards for Christian Education Settings (Swaner and Erdvig 2018), which we developed as a companion for Christian school settings. These standards address an additional four core areas that are critical to service-learning in Christian school settings: (1) Christ-likeness; (2) worldview development; (3) servant-leadership; and (4) lifelong service. These two sets of standards are presented below, followed by suggestions as to how to utilize the standards in practice.

The K–12 Service-Learning Standards for Quality Practice (National Youth Leadership Council 2008; reprinted with permission).

Meaningful Service
Service-learning actively engages participants in meaningful and personally relevant service activities.

Indicators:

1. Service-learning experiences are appropriate to participant ages and developmental abilities.

2. Service-learning addresses issues that are personally relevant to the participants.

3. Service-learning provides participants with interesting and engaging service activities.

4. Service-learning encourages participants to understand their service experiences in the context of the underlying societal issues being addressed.

5. Service-learning leads to attainable and visible outcomes that are valued by those being served.

Link to Curriculum

Service-learning is intentionally used as an instructional strategy to meet learning goals and/or content standards.

Indicators:

1. Service-learning has clearly articulated learning goals.

2. Service-learning is aligned with the academic and/or programmatic curriculum.

3. Service-learning helps participants learn how to transfer knowledge and skills from one setting to another.

4. Service-learning that takes place in schools is formally recognized in school board policies and student records.

Reflection

Service-learning incorporates multiple challenging reflection activities that are ongoing and that prompt deep thinking and analysis about oneself and one's relationship to society.

1. Service-learning reflection includes a variety of verbal, written, artistic, and nonverbal activities to demonstrate understanding and changes in participants' knowledge, skills, and/or attitudes.

2. Service-learning reflection occurs before, during, and after the service experience.

3. Service-learning reflection prompts participants to think deeply about complex community problems and alternative solutions.

4. Service-learning reflection encourages participants to examine their preconceptions and assumptions in order to explore and understand their roles and responsibilities as citizens.

5. Service-learning reflection encourages participants to examine a variety of social and civic issues related to their service-learning experience so that participants understand connections to public policy and civic life.

Diversity

Service-learning promotes understanding of diversity and mutual respect among all participants.

Indicators:

1. Service-learning helps participants identify and analyze different points of view to gain understanding of multiple perspectives.

2. Service-learning helps participants develop

interpersonal skills in conflict resolution and group decision making.

3. Service-learning helps participants actively seek to understand and value the diverse backgrounds and perspectives of those offering and receiving service.

4. Service-learning encourages participants to recognize and overcome stereotypes.

Youth Voice

Service-learning provides youth with a strong voice in planning, implementing, and evaluating service-learning experiences with guidance from adults.

Indicators:

1. Service-learning engages youth in generating ideas during the planning, implementation, and evaluation processes.

2. Service-learning involves youth in the decision-making process throughout the service-learning experiences.

3. Service-learning involves youth and adults in creating an environment that supports trust and open expression of ideas.

4. Service-learning promotes acquisition of knowledge and skills to enhance youth leadership and decision making.

5. Service-learning involves youth in evaluating the quality and effectiveness of the service-learning

experience.

Partnerships
Service-learning partnerships are collaborative, mutually beneficial, and address community needs.

Indicators:
1. Service-learning involves a variety of partners, including youth, educators, families, community members, community-based organizations, and/or businesses.

2. Service-learning partnerships are characterized by frequent and regular communication to keep all partners well-informed about activities and progress.

3. Service-learning partners collaborate to establish a shared vision and set common goals to address community needs.

4. Service-learning partners collaboratively develop and implement action plans to meet specified goals.

5. Service-learning partners share knowledge and understanding of school and community assets and needs, and view each other as valued resources.

Progress Monitoring
Service-learning engages participants in an ongoing process to assess the quality of implementation and progress toward meeting specified goals, and uses results for improvement and sustainability.

Indicators:

1. Service-learning participants collect evidence of progress toward meeting specific service goals and learning outcomes from multiple sources throughout the service-learning experience.

2. Service-learning participants collect evidence of the quality of service-learning implementation from multiple sources throughout the service-learning experience.

3. Service-learning participants use evidence to improve service-learning experiences.

4. Service-learning participants communicate evidence of progress toward goals and outcomes with the broader community, including policy-makers and education leaders, to deepen service-learning understanding and ensure that high quality practices are sustained.

Duration and Intensity
Service-learning has sufficient duration and intensity to address community needs and meet specified outcomes.

Indicators:

1. Service-learning experiences include the processes of investigating community needs, preparing for service, action, reflection, demonstration of learning and impacts, and celebration.

2. Service-learning is conducted during concentrated blocks of time across a period of several weeks or

months.

3. Service-learning experiences provide enough time
    to address identified community needs and achieve
    learning outcomes.

**K–12 Supplemental Service-Learning Standards for Christian
Education Settings** (Swaner and Erdvig 2018)

Christ-likeness
**Service-learning encourages the growth of Christ-likeness in
students, as students learn to serve others as Christ served.**

Indicators:
1. Service-learning provides direct, biblically based
    instruction on Christ-likeness as a goal for every
    believer.

2. Service-learning helps students learn to identify
    and meet practical needs in the community, while
    representing Christ in a loving and compassionate
    manner to those being served.

3. Service-learning harnesses the discipleship process
    and spiritual disciplines to engage students in a
    process of cognitive, affective, and behavioral change
    toward Christ-likeness.

4. Service-learning provides students with structured
    opportunities for ongoing reflection on their growth
    in Christ-likeness.

Servant Leadership

Service-learning provides opportunities for students to develop a range of leadership skills, as well as a vision for utilizing those skills as servant leaders.

Indicators:

1. Service-learning includes direct instruction on the concept of servant leadership, including examples from the life and ministry of Christ.

2. Service-learning provides structured opportunities for reflection on the concept of servant leadership and how it relates to students' experiences.

3. Service-learning experiences allow students to practice and hone their organizational, communication, and problem-solving skills.

4. Service-learning provides self-evaluative activities for students to gauge their development as servant leaders.

Worldview Development

Service-learning promotes biblical worldview development and a view of service as an expression of God's restorative work in the world.

Indicators:

1. Service-learning provides direct instruction to students regarding their role as God's image-bearers who are created for service, in keeping with Ephesians 2:10 (ESV): "For we are his workmanship, created in Christ Jesus for good works, which God prepared beforehand, that we should walk in them."

2. Service-learning includes opportunities for students to discover how they personally fit—and can use their unique talents and gifts to serve—in God's enduring story (of creation, fall, redemption, and restoration).

3. Service-learning provides students with structured opportunities for reflection on their worldview development, and how they "live out" that worldview as Christ-followers and as they serve others.

Lifelong Service
Service-learning promotes an orientation toward lifelong service.

Indicators:
1. Service-learning provides direct instruction on the importance of serving others as an expression of God's restorative work in the world (in keeping with God's enduring story of creation, fall, redemption, and restoration).

2. Service-learning provides structured opportunities for discussion and reflection on how the believer is called to serve one's family, church, community, and workplace in response to God's love.

3. Service-learning encourages the development of students' personal identity as servants and agents of God's restorative work in all arenas of life.

Suggestions for Using the Standards
We have found both sets of standards to be helpful in a number of ways when working with schools, whether they

are starting off with service-learning or in the process of implementing projects. These include using the standards: as a learning resource, planning aid, and evaluative tool.

Using Standards as a Learning Resource

Often faculty have difficulty envisioning what service-learning entails because they find it hard to hold so many instructional components—course content, service, and reflection—in their thinking at the same time. This is particularly true if they have not had any previous exposure to service-learning. In addition to concrete examples of service-learning projects (such as those offered in this book), the standards can be used to help faculty imagine what service-learning might look like and understand the key components of a successful project. While certainly faculty can review the standards on their own,

Service-Learning Snapshot:
When a high school history teacher found out his class would be doing service-learning for the first time in the following academic year, he was initially apprehensive. Along with two other teachers from his grade level, he attended an all-day work session to begin planning. As he read through the standards for service-learning, he began to envision a project that partnered with a local church to serve international refugees in his city. The project would tie in with course content on immigration in the United States, and help students to learn how to love their neighbors through practical service (Luke 10:25–37). The more he thought about and discussed his idea for a project in the context of understanding the standards, his concerns decreased and he left the work session excited about the idea—with high motivation to develop it further.

we've found it most helpful when faculty are homogenously grouped—by grade level, division, or department—and examine the standards together during a planned professional development day. Guiding questions (such as those at the end of this chapter) can be used to generate group discussion about how the standards might apply to faculty members' own classrooms. Reviewing the standards as a group also provides the opportunity for faculty to develop a list of questions that need either more consideration or direct input from school leaders. Sometimes we've heard educators describe reviewing the standards as a way to "gather our ignorance on the subject"—meaning to determine what they don't yet know about service-learning, what they need to know, and how they are going to acquire that knowledge.

Using Standards as a Planning Aid

Faculty are typically accustomed to considering standards when they develop curriculum, so it should not be too much of a stretch for most faculty to use the service-learning standards as guidelines for project design. Standards can be incorporated in any planning sessions for service-learning, and faculty can be asked to document how they are linking the standards to how they are formulating their specific projects. To this end, we provide a helpful reflection exercise—for both teachers and school leaders, below—for thinking through how standards can inform service-learning planning.

Designing Projects to Meet Service-Learning Standards

Standard	Design Question	**Design Answer** (provide <u>specific examples</u> of how the project will meet this standard)
Meaningful Service (NYLC 2008)	How will the project actively engage participants in meaningful and personally relevant service activities?	
Link to Curriculum (NYLC 2008)	How will the project meet the learning goals and/or content standards of the course?	
Reflection (NYLC 2008)	Does the service-learning experience involve multiple and ongoing challenging reflection activities that prompt deep thinking and analysis about oneself and one's relationship to society?	
Diversity (NYLC 2008)	Does the project promote understanding of diversity and mutual respect among all participants?	
Youth Voice (NYLC 2008)	Do students have a strong voice in planning, implementing, and evaluating the service-learning experience, with guidance from adults?	
Partnerships (NYLC 2008)	Are the partnerships developed for this project collaborative and mutually beneficial, and do they address community needs?	

Standard	Design Question	Design Answer (provide _specific examples_ of how the project will meet this standard)
Progress Monitoring (NYLC 2008)	Are participants engaged in an ongoing process to assess the quality of implementation and progress toward meeting specified goals, and use results for improvement and sustainability?	
Duration and Intensity (NYLC 2008)	Is the project of sufficient duration and intensity to address community needs and meet specified outcomes?	
Christ-likeness (Swaner and Erdvig 2018)	Does the project encourage the growth of Christ-likeness in students, and are students learning to serve others as Christ served?	
Servant Leadership (Swaner and Erdvig 2018)	Do students have opportunity to develop a range of leadership skills, as well as a vision for utilizing those skills as servant leaders?	
Worldview Development (Swaner and Erdvig 2018)	Does the project promote the development of a biblical worldview, and an understanding of service as an expression of God's restorative work in the world?	
Lifelong Service (Swaner and Erdvig 2018)	Does the experience promote an orientation toward lifelong service in all arenas of life?	

In addition to being helpful for planning projects, the service-learning standards can be incorporated into the school's core academic documents and processes as a way to further embed service-learning in the curriculum. In our various accreditation visits to schools over the years, we've found that curriculum guides and lesson plans are often linked to content standards at the K–12 level; ideally, standards related to service-learning can also be incorporated in those guides and plans as well. To begin this process, the next chapter includes a scope and sequence worksheet for service-learning that incorporates "learning standards" in the first column. Incorporating the standards presented in this chapter within the scope and sequence will help faculty to think through how service-learning experiences not only connect with course content, but also are in alignment with those standards. Finally, service-learning standards can also be incorporated into a school's existing curricular review process, with service-learning outcomes linked to the school's overall expected student outcomes (ESOs).

Overall, the closer service-learning (and related standards) can be tied to the core structures and processes of the school, the more integrated it will become for faculty and students alike. To this end, instructional leaders need to continually ask, "How can we integrate service-learning into what we're doing right now?"—whether in professional development opportunities, curricular review and planning, or schoolwide assessment.

Using Standards as an Evaluative Tool

Service-learning standards can also be used to support evaluation efforts. Although chapter 6 presents a comprehensive framework for evaluating service-learning, it's worth mentioning the importance of standards to evaluation here. Simply stated, standards provide an objective set of criteria for determining whether and to what degree service-learning projects have been successful. Lacking standards by which to evaluate projects, it's anybody's (and everybody's!) guess as to how well the project went. One way to incorporate the standards into evaluation is to ask three basic questions on (at least) an annual basis:

1. Did the project meet the standards for service-learning?
2. How or how not?
3. How do we know? (e.g., what evidences do we have?)

For schools looking to incorporate the standards on a deeper level, they can be woven into the evaluation plan for service-learning. (This concept will be discussed further in chapter 6). In the meantime, it's key to remember that standards can be useful for all stages of service-learning, from planning to implementation to evaluation.

Case-Story: Addressing Disaster Preparedness and Conservation through Life Science

A middle school life science teacher observed that many students had difficulty mastering key topics in the course. They also frequently complained that they didn't understand how they would use these topics "in real life." The teacher decided to reorient the content of the course—particularly units on natural disasters and conservation—toward a service-learning project that involved building homes for families in the next county after a widespread forest fire devastated several neighborhoods there. The outcomes for the project included the academic outcomes already in the curriculum guide for the course for these units, but the teacher added that students would: (1) learn about proper stewardship of God's creation; (2) enact that learning through conservation and forest fire prevention efforts; (3) learn about practical ways to serve those who have been the victims of natural disasters; and (4) develop an orientation toward serving others as a key part of both their worldview and identity as Christians.

The teacher had experience working with a national volunteer agency that constructed homes for families in need of housing. This agency had a building site underway in the neighboring county, in a neighborhood that had been affected by the forest fires. While students were not able to participate in all elements of the build (due to their status as minors and liability and insurance limitations), they were able to visit the build site on a monthly basis during the school year and assist with landscaping, unloading materials from trucks, and priming and painting materials before they were installed in the home. Through this process, they learned about fire prevention measures in landscaping and construction. They were also able to take various environmental samples (e.g., soil, plant life, aridity) at the building site, which could inform their understanding of the risks for fires in the area.

Outside of the planned service trips, many students also arranged on their own to return with their families or youth groups to continue working at the site on weekends. Students also held various fundraisers at the school and in their churches to raise money for gift cards for the family so they could purchase furnishings and home items upon moving in. The class was able to meet the future homeowners, who visited the site frequently and interacted with volunteers. At the completion of the build, the students were able to take part in the ceremony and celebration when the family took possession of the home.

The teacher scheduled a "debrief lab" following each of the trips to the building site. During each lab, students worked in pairs to examine the data they collected at the site and work on problems assigned by the teacher. Each pair was then grouped with another pair of students to compare findings and results, as well as to discuss the connection of the concept being studied and the work at the building site. Each student documented the day's work in a lab journal and then was assigned a structured reflection question regarding the service experience for homework. Prompts for journals directly addressed the course's targeted outcomes, such as stewardship, conservation, serving those in need, and developing an identity and worldview that included serving others.

Student learning was assessed through unit tests, lab grades, and lab journal response grades. As this was the science teacher's first year at the school, student assessment data was not available for previous years. However, via comparison of survey data, the teacher found that both students and parents noted higher levels of student engagement and interest in the course than in prior years, when service-learning was not part of the course.

Next Steps

1. If service-learning projects are *already underway* at your school, use the exercise in this chapter ("Designing Projects to Meet Service-Learning Standards") to assess their alignment with the standards presented in this chapter.

2. If your school has *not yet implemented* any service-learning projects, develop a hypothetical project idea and use the exercise provided in this chapter ("Designing Projects to Meet Service-Learning Standards") to flesh out the idea further.

Questions for Discussion

1. How could becoming familiar with the service-learning standards help inform service-learning at our school?

2. In what specific venues (e.g., meetings, processes) at our school might the standards be useful?

3. How can our school use the standards in the planning process for service-learning?

4
Designing Service-Learning

Successful service-learning at a Christian school begins with a well-thought-out plan crafted by those who will be implementing service-learning. This means teachers must identify and articulate key elements of service-learning, including the project's outcomes, scope and sequence, evaluation, logistics, and budget. This chapter provides a process and a useful template for project planning for teachers, while chapter 5 suggests ways that school leaders can support service-learning.

Once Christian school educators grasp the potential value of service-learning to fulfilling their school's mission, they often are eager to get started right away. But we have seen an interesting phenomenon at many schools: school leaders and faculty start off excited by a new pedagogy, but their ability to execute change in classroom practice is hampered by the tyranny of the urgent, a lack of time for reflection, or sheer inertia (a.k.a. "old habits die hard"). We have come to largely attribute this to an old adage: "those who fail to plan, plan to fail." Our goal in this chapter (and the next) is to help readers avoid this outcome by walking through the steps of planning for service-learning. Ultimately, successful planning will help teachers and schools to realize the promise of service-learning through successful projects.

How to Get Started

It may be tempting to begin thinking about service-learning by dreaming of all the wonderful ways students can get out into the community to help others. The difficulty with this approach is that, typically, one of two things results: a project that focuses too heavily on service, and does not connect directly or strongly enough to the curriculum; or a project that involves active learning and student engagement, but that fails to incorporate reflection or authentic service adequately. The reason is that service-learning, as discussed in earlier chapters, is a complex pedagogy that involves many moving parts (in terms of people and sites of learning). It is difficult to assemble those parts into a successful service-learning project without careful thought.

The best place to start searching for service-learning ideas is the *curriculum itself*, with the reason that service-learning projects must be grounded in the existing learning objectives, as well as scope and sequence of courses. Service-learning works best when it naturally flows from the content being taught as opposed to being forced into the curriculum. A good way to start is for teachers to examine their course content and identify units, topics, or themes that may benefit from a more active learning approach and/or learning experiences outside of the classroom. Sometimes these can be areas with which students have difficulty in the course, or that could use revamping after many years of being taught the same way. Some reflection questions to ask of the curriculum include:

- Which themes, units, and lessons have obvious practical, real-world applications?
- What content in this course could better be grasped by students if it involved hands-on learning?
- In what professions would a person use the themes and content of this course?
- How might God use a theme or topic in this course to meet people's needs?

In answering these questions, it is also important to consider what assignments, activities, field trips, and other course elements could be "swapped" with service-learning. This is because service-learning won't work as an "add-on," as it is too time- and resource-intensive to simply wedge into an already packed instructional schedule. Moreover, for it to be meaningful for students, service-learning needs to be an integral part of their experience in the course. Thus, teachers need to think not only of where to anchor service-learning in the course content, but also how they will make *sufficient room* for it during the year.

Once potential areas of the curriculum are identified, it is helpful to go back to read and reflect on the *service-learning standards* presented in chapter 3 (the National Youth Leadership Council K–12 Service-Learning Standards for Quality Practice, and the K–12 Supplemental Service-Learning Standards for Christian Education settings). This will help teachers frame all of their planning in terms of high-quality service-learning. It's easy to miss the distinctives that separate service-learning from traditional community service projects, mission trips, or even hands-on field trips. As we've discussed in earlier chapters, while all of these experiences are valid and valuable, they are not in themselves service-learning. Carefully reviewing the standards at this point can help set the stage correctly, from the start.

We've also found *collaboration* to be extremely helpful in this initial stage of planning. For example, many times when we've led planning sessions with small groups of teachers they served as sounding boards for one another, by bouncing ideas back and forth until they begin to crystallize. As individuals share ideas about areas of their courses that may be taught effectively through service-learning, they can gain clarity and new insights through the questions and input from colleagues. It's not uncommon for ideas in one discipline or content area to spark new ideas in other areas. As their ideas develop, teachers can work in pairs or small groups to begin recording their thoughts (a tool for this stage in planning, *Brainstorming Service-Learning Projects*, is included in chapter 7 of this guidebook).

Service-Learning Snapshot:
One high school physics class planned and executed a successful service-learning project by generating a proposal for their local town board to address a dangerous intersection in the community. The idea was sparked by a conversation between the teacher and a fellow church member, who happened to be a town board official. The teacher explained how the class was looking to use their understanding of physics to help serve the community. As the two brainstormed possible areas of need, the traffic problem rose to the top of the list of projects, particularly because the intersection was within walking distance from the school, and the students in the class were familiar with the problem already. As part of the project, the students spent time each month serving with the town highway crew. They assisted with inspecting roads, monitoring traffic flow, and replacing signs, which helped them to become familiar with the solutions available to address traffic safety. Their proposal to the town board was successful, but the class felt the relationships they developed with the highway crew—and the opportunity to demonstrate God's love through service, in the context of those relationships—was the most valuable part of the service-learning experience.

Identifying Community Sites

The next step in the planning process is to identify sites in the community that may have needs suited to the project idea. This task can be daunting for many reasons, and teachers often start out fearing they will not be able to find a community site where their students can serve. Sometimes finding appropriate service sites can be a challenge, especially if the Christian school does not regularly engage with the broader community in which it is situated.

Often a good place to start is to connect with a local church or ministry outreach center. Many local churches will have significant outreach ministries that may be able to connect a teacher and class with legitimate community needs. For example, some churches operate food pantries, senior citizen programs, ministries to single mothers, or various ministries to at-risk youth. Most areas also have independent parachurch ministries that focus on specific populations, such as rescue missions, crisis pregnancy centers, and youth mentoring organizations. These faith-based organizations can all be good places to identify a need that can be met through a service-learning project.

However, it is wise to also consider choosing service sites outside of church and parachurch settings, as doing so can connect the school and students with the local community in unique and powerful ways. Local governments, chambers of commerce, rotary clubs, libraries, and other community organizations are all potential sources of information about needs that may work well for a service-learning project. Parks commissions, animal rescue organizations, and nature conservancies are also good sites to consider. Contact with local chapters of veterans' organizations, chambers of commerce, and other community or fraternal organizations may provide leads. In some cases, local businesses, medical offices or centers, nonprofits, and legislators' offices may be engaged in charitable or volunteer activities, which could be parlayed into service-learning projects for school students. The benefits of partnering with these kinds of organizations are that many: students gain experience serving outside of the church; interact in meaningful ways with people who are often not believers; and learn how to engage in God's restorative work as an ambassador of Christ to the world.

Regardless of the setting, and whether or not the school has an existing connection with a contact person, it's important for teachers to be well-prepared for an initial conversation with a potential site. Preparation includes being clear on what the teacher is asking for and being realistic with what a project might look like. We've found that leaders in organizations generally enjoy connecting with youth and children, but they often cannot accurately picture what a successful service project might look like. Keeping in mind the value of establishing relationships with people (and not just doing a quick one-time service project), a good place to start is to ask them what ongoing needs they have and if they would be open to a discussion about how a group of students from the school may be able to help them. Explain the heart behind service-learning and how the purpose is to help students connect meaningfully with the community.

> **Service-Learning Snapshot:**
> *Time spent in thinking through potential projects from many different logistical angles is not wasted. A middle school teacher wanted to partner with a local animal shelter for a service-learning project focused on science and learning to be stewards of God's creation. Plans were made and dates were chosen before the teacher discovered that her students, due to insurance rules, were too young to serve at the site. Some simple initial questions about the feasibility of serving with that site likely would have saved significant time and would have prevented frustration and disappointment for the teacher and students.*

Asking questions about logistics (what the students will do, how often they can visit, and with whom will they interact) is important, with the goal of determining whether or not the site is actually a good "fit" for students. The site needs to be chosen with realistic expectations of what the students can actually do, as well as what they are allowed to do (legally or otherwise). We know of a few situations where teachers went to great lengths planning a significant project, only to find out that the site they had in mind couldn't actually accommodate the students for legal, liability, or space-related issues. Some simple investigation prior to in-depth planning can help to avoid lost time and disappointment.

Involving Students in Planning

It is important to note that teachers should not merely come up with a fully-developed project that gives students little opportunity to have a voice in planning and decision-making. While it is virtually impossible in a K–12 environment to give over *all* planning to the students, teachers should actively look for every opportunity to involve students in the decision-making process about what to do and how to do it (this relates to the service-learning standard of incorporating youth voice, as discussed in chapter 3). The older the students are, the more voice and responsibility they should have in planning their service-learning experiences. Thus, teachers in the upper high school grades will involve students in planning to a greater degree than in lower elementary, but all teachers can give some responsibility over to the students.

We've observed a few barriers when it comes to asking teachers to incorporate meaningful student involvement in service-learning. First, teachers are busy, and it can be easier to do all the planning themselves. A teacher who is highly organized can find it cumbersome and inconvenient to leave gaps in the planning for students to fill. Second, teachers can have a hard time facilitating planning discussions with students. The concept that students should be able to speak into the curriculum and class activities can be a foreign one, and unfortunately, as adults, we often don't trust that children and youth have good ideas.

However, effective service-learning overcomes these obstacles and maximizes students' involvement in the planning, implementation, and evaluation of projects. Teachers can accomplish this by establishing the basic structure and boundaries of service-learning. For younger students, this can mean giving them a set of options from which to make choices. Older students can be given a set of parameters within which to develop ideas and solutions of their own. Student input can also be sought throughout the project by asking probing questions like:

- What do you think we should do next in order to prepare for this project?
- What kinds of things do you think would be most helpful for us to do on site, out of these choices of activities?
- What do you think would be the most effective way to do this specific task?
- When we encountered that obstacle or difficulty, how should we have handled it? What should we do next time?

In addition, students can be given responsibilities for various parts of the project in age-appropriate ways. For example, older students can assist with logistics for trips to a site and making phone calls to the community partner, while younger students can help to identify what kinds of supplies should be taken to a site.

From an outcomes perspective, allowing for student involvement in planning has a number of benefits. Service-learning facilitates the development of many "soft" skills including those that are necessary for leadership. To illustrate this, it's helpful to imagine a Christian school in which students experience authentic service-learning at every grade level from grades K through 12. Students begin with simple projects in kindergarten that expose them to the joy of serving others along with learning phonics and arithmetic; from the very start of their formal education, they learn by serving others. Then, throughout the rest of their school years, meaningful service and connections with their community are normal, expected ways of learning. As students progress toward high school, the projects in which they participate become more complex, and they see firsthand the impact they have in the lives of the people in their community. And all along the way, teachers give them incrementally more responsibility in the planning and execution of their projects.

In this illustration, by the time these students reach their senior year, they would have considerable experience with service-learning because it was woven into the very fabric of their education. This being the case, seniors in such a school could essentially take the lead in planning and implementing service-learning, with their teachers as guides and resource-people. In this way leadership becomes the "hidden curriculum" of service-learning, when teachers allow students the opportunity to share responsibility for planning and implementing their experiences.

Service-Learning Case Story: Honoring Those Who Served through World History

An eleventh-grade history teacher integrated service-learning into the curriculum on world history, by focusing on the concept of war throughout time. The teacher wanted the class to not only learn about war throughout human history, but also to gain a full appreciation of the great sacrifices and losses made in war. An important part of the course was discussing moral questions related to war—including exploring biblical views on the morality of war (debating whether and when war is justified)—and discussing ways that Christians should respond to the human needs created by war. In addition to the outcomes identified in the curriculum guide for the class, these larger questions helped to shape the desired service-learning outcomes.

The teacher's home church had a thriving veterans' ministry, headed by the community pastor. The ministry held monthly veterans' breakfasts at the church that were well attended. As a service experience, students assisted in preparing and serving the veterans breakfast at the church four times during the year (once per quarter). During the breakfasts, students also sat at tables with the veterans and had opportunity to dialogue with them about their experiences.

The ministry also maintained a roster of both church and community members who were veterans and who needed some form of assistance on a regular basis (e.g., transportation to medical appointments, house and lawn maintenance, food supplies and prepared meals, and visitation). Each student was required to log ten hours during the school year in providing direct assistance to a veteran, which was arranged through the ministry. (Students' parents were required to accompany students and/or provide needed transportation.) Finally, the students themselves developed and led several fundraisers throughout the year, including bake sales and a 5K race, to raise money for the veterans' ministry.

Students kept a weekly journal in which they responded to structured reflection questions provided by the teacher, many of which focused on students' views of war and how Christians should respond to the needs created by war. These journal entries were submitted online to the teacher as well as posted on the class's online learning management system. Students were required to read each other's journals and reply constructively to at least two other students' journals every week. In addition, after each service activity, the teacher spent the next class leading group discussions to debrief students' experiences and connect what they learned to the curriculum. Through these activities, the students came to describe their interactions with veterans as putting a "human face and voice" on the course content and the larger moral questions they were exploring.

Assessment for the service-learning project included grading of students' journal submissions and comments in the class's online learning management system, as well as a culminating paper in the last quarter that synthesized their learning from the year. The teacher created a rubric to grade these papers based on their level of analysis and integration of learning, and found that students who participated in service-learning scored better than previous years' students on the culminating paper. Finally, students created group projects in which they designed their own programs for meeting veterans' needs at their own churches. They presented these projects to the class, with the community pastor (in charge of the veterans' ministry) present to offer encouragement and constructive criticism.

Writing a Formal Plan

While brainstorming, collaborating, and involving students are all important components of the planning process, we have found that a structured planning process and document—or template—is needed to help teachers break down the task of designing service-learning experiences. The remainder of this chapter provides a template for project planning that has been developed for, tested at, and used successfully in multiple K–12 Christian schools.

The template uses a series of questions to help faculty identify important elements of service-learning. These include the desired outcomes, the scope and sequence for both the content and service experiences, how the project will be evaluated, and logistical and budgeting considerations. Each section of the template not only solicits important information about project design, but also asks faculty to reflect on their curriculum and how they will integrate service-learning. The final part of the template is a reflection activity that faculty will complete—to encourage them to engage in the same kind of reflection in which their students will need in order for service-learning to be successful.

The Service-Learning Project Planning Template
Swaner and Erdvig (2018)

Faculty Name(s):   Grade/Subject:

Proposed Project Title: Project Year:

PROJECT OVERVIEW

1. Provide a brief description of your project (a.k.a. your "elevator speech").

2. Identify the specific community to be served.

3. Identify the major content subjects/areas and units into which the project will be incorporated.

LEARNING OBJECTIVES

4. Identify the major learning goals for students (in other words, how this experience should impact students). Please list at least 5 goals.

   a.

   b.

   c.

   d.

   e.

5. Identify the major service goals for the community being served (in other words, how this experience should impact the community/those being served). Please list at least 3 goals.

   a.

   b.

   c.

6. Describe how the project addresses the goals of Christian education, specifically:

a) promoting Christ-likeness in students

b) helping students develop a biblical worldview

c) teaching students how to be servant leaders

d) helping students understand their role as agents of restoration in God's enduring story

e) other related goals

7. Describe how the project will help students to develop personally, in terms of discovering and developing their unique talents and gifts.

PROJECT SCOPE AND SEQUENCE

On the following pages, provide your scope and sequence for your service-learning project. *It is expected that as your project develops further and/or you finalize logistics for the project, you may need to make adjustments.* However please provide as much detail as you can at this point.

Below you will find a list of the column headings for the scope and sequence chart, along with an explanation of what kinds of information to include for each:

- **Unit/Dates and Learning Standards**: Identify the specific course unit and the approximate dates for the unit, as well as content learning standards and the service-learning standards (by the National Youth Leadership Council 2008, and Swaner and Erdvig 2018, provided immediately following the scope and sequence chart, for reference).

- **Learning Activities**: List the learning activities within the unit. Describe the specific lesson plans within the unit that will incorporate the service-learning project.

- **Service Experience**: Identify the service experience that will accompany the unit. Note that not every unit will have a corresponding service activity; rather, aim to incorporate a service experience at least once a quarter.

- **Biblical Integration**: Describe how you will integrate Scripture and biblical principles into the service-learning experience for this unit. Describe how the experience/unit will help students grow in Christ-likeness, worldview development, servant leadership, and lifelong service.

- **Reflection Methods**: List the methods you will use to promote reflection (with the ultimate goal of connecting in-class learning with the service experience). Suggestions include journals, facilitated discussion, diagrams/artwork, storytelling, etc.

- **Assessment Methods**: List the assessments for the unit that will address the service-learning component. This could include papers, tests, graded journals, projects, presentations, etc.

Please note that your planning should consider the progressive stages of service-learning, as follows:

I. Introduction to Service-Learning

In the beginning of the year, the class will need to spend time becoming "oriented" to the service experience. This will include investigating the problem(s) to be addressed, exploring together the possible solutions, and providing guidelines/expectations/instructions for actual service. It is ideal to schedule a weekly classroom timeslot for the service-learning activities.

II. Engaging in Service-Learning

This is the "doing" phase and likely the longest stage, when students are engaged in learning content in the classroom, serving the community, and reflecting on that service whenever they return to the classroom. Remember that for the service experiences to be impactful, they must happen regularly in the year. As a rule of thumb, you will want to try to incorporate a service experience at least once a quarter.

III. Wrapping Up the Experience

Units toward the end of the year should include wrap-up activities, such as celebrations, capstone events, or presentations. Be sure to think about ways to help students reflect on their learning overall and to bring the project to a sense of closure. Wherever it is possible, student work and learning should be shared with others (e.g., inviting community participants, parents, others at the school, etc.).

Unit/Dates, Learning Standards	Learning Activities	Service Experience (if applicable)	Biblical Integration	Reflection Methods	Assessment Methods

Unit/Dates, Learning Standards	Learning Activities	Service Experience (if applicable)	Biblical Integration	Reflection Methods	Assessment Methods

Meaningful Service
Service-learning actively engages participants in meaningful and personally relevant service activities.

Indicators:
1. Service-learning experiences are appropriate to participant ages and developmental abilities.
2. Service-learning addresses issues that are personally relevant to the participants.
3. Service-learning provides participants with interesting and engaging activities.
4. Service-learning encourages participants to understand their service experiences in the context of the underlying societal issues being addressed.
5. Service-learning leads to attainable and visible outcomes that are valued by those being served.

Link to Curriculum
Service-learning is intentionally used as an instructional strategy to meet learning goals and/or content standards.

Indicators:
1. Service-learning has clearly articulated learning goals.
2. Service-learning is aligned with the academic and/or programmatic curriculum.
3. Service-learning helps participants learn how to transfer knowledge and skills from one setting to another.
4. Service-learning that takes place in schools is formally recognized in school board policies and student records.

Reflection

Service-learning incorporates multiple challenging reflection activities that are ongoing and that prompt deep thinking and analysis about oneself and one's relationship to society.

Indicators:
1. Service-learning reflection includes a variety of verbal, written, artistic, and nonverbal activities to demonstrate understanding and changes in participants' knowledge, skills, and/or attitudes.
2. Service-learning reflection occurs before, during, and after the service experience.
3. Service-learning reflection prompts participants to think deeply about complex community problems and alternative solutions.
4. Service-learning reflection encourages participants to examine their preconceptions and assumptions in order to explore and understand their roles and responsibilities as citizens.
5. Service-learning reflection encourages participants to examine a variety of social and civic issues related to their service-learning experience so that participants understand connections to public policy and civic life.

Diversity

Service-learning promotes understanding of diversity and mutual respect among all participants.

Indicators:
1. Service-learning helps participants identify and analyze different points of view to gain understanding of multiple perspectives.
2. Service-learning helps participants develop interpersonal skills in conflict resolution and group decision making.
3. Service-learning helps participants actively seek to understand and value the diverse backgrounds and perspectives of those offering and receiving service.
4. Service-learning encourages participants to recognize and overcome stereotypes.

Youth Voice
Service-learning provides youth with a strong voice in planning, implementing, and evaluating service-learning experiences with guidance from adults.

Indicators:
1. Service-learning engages youth in generating ideas during the planning, implementation, and evaluation processes.
2. Service-learning involves youth in the decision-making process throughout the service-learning experiences.
3. Service-learning involves youth and adults in creating an environment that supports trust and open expression of ideas.
4. Service-learning promotes acquisition of knowledge and skills to enhance youth leadership and decision making.
5. Service-learning involves youth in evaluating the quality and effectiveness of the service-learning experience.

Partnerships
Service-learning partnerships are collaborative, mutually beneficial, and address community needs.

Indicators:
1. Service-learning involves a variety of partners, including youth, educators, families, community members, community-based organizations, and/or businesses.
2. Service-learning partnerships are characterized by frequent and regular communication to keep all partners well-informed about activities and progress.
3. Service-learning partners collaborate to establish a shared vision and set common goals to address community needs.
4. Service-learning partners collaboratively develop and implement action plans to meet specified goals.
5. Service-learning partners share knowledge and understanding of school and community assets and needs, and view each other as valued resources.

Progress Monitoring

Service-learning engages participants in an ongoing process to assess the quality of implementation and progress toward meeting specified goals, and uses results for improvement and sustainability.

Indicators:

1. Service-learning participants collect evidence of progress toward meeting specific service goals and learning outcomes from multiple sources throughout the service-learning experience.
2. Service-learning participants collect evidence of the quality of service-learning implementation from multiple sources throughout the service-learning experience.
3. Service-learning participants use evidence to improve service-learning experiences.
4. Service-learning participants communicate evidence of progress toward goals and outcomes with the broader community, including policy-makers and education leaders, to deepen service-learning understanding and ensure that high quality practices are sustained.

Duration and Intensity

Service-learning has sufficient duration and intensity to address community needs and meet specified outcomes.

Indicators:

1. Service-learning experiences include the processes of investigating community needs, preparing for service, action, reflection, demonstration of learning and impacts, and celebration.
2. Service-learning is conducted during concentrated blocks of time across a period of several weeks or months.
3. Service-learning experiences provide enough time to address identified community needs and achieve learning outcomes.

Christ-likeness
Service-learning encourages the growth of Christ-likeness in students, as students learn to serve others as Christ served.

Indicators:
1. Service-learning provides direct, biblically based instruction on Christ-likeness as a goal for every believer.
2. Service-learning helps students learn to identify and meet practical needs in the community, while representing Christ in a loving and compassionate manner to those being served.
3. Service-learning harnesses the discipleship process and spiritual disciplines to engage students in a process of cognitive, affective, and behavioral change toward Christ-likeness.
4. Service-learning provides students with structured opportunities for ongoing reflection on their growth in Christ-likeness.

Servant Leadership
Service-learning provides opportunities for students to develop a range of leadership skills, as well as a vision for utilizing those skills as servant leaders.

Indicators:
1. Service-learning includes direct instruction on the concept of servant leadership, including examples from the life and ministry of Christ.
2. Service-learning provides structured opportunities for reflection on the concept of servant leadership and how it relates to students' experiences.
3. Service-learning experiences allow students to practice and hone their organizational, communication, and problem-solving skills.
4. Service-learning provides self-evaluative activities for students to gauge their development as servant leaders.

Worldview Development
Service-learning promotes biblical worldview development and a view of service as an expression of God's restorative work in the world.

Indicators:
1. Service-learning provides direct instruction to students regarding their role as God's image-bearers who are created for service, in keeping with Ephesians 2:10 (ESV): "For we are his workmanship, created in Christ Jesus for good works, which God prepared beforehand, that we should walk in them."
2. Service-learning includes opportunities for students to discover how they personally fit—and can use their unique talents and gifts to serve—in God's enduring story (of creation, fall, redemption, and restoration).
3. Service-learning provides students with structured opportunities for reflection on their worldview development and how they "live out" that worldview as Christ-followers and as they serve others.

Lifelong Service
Service-learning promotes an orientation toward lifelong service.

Indicators:
1. Service-learning provides direct instruction on the importance of serving others as an expression of God's restorative work in the world (in keeping with God's enduring story of creation, fall, redemption, and restoration).
2. Service-learning provides structured opportunities for discussion and reflection on how the believer is called to serve one's family, church, community, and workplace in response to God's love.
3. Service-learning encourages the development of students' personal identity as servants and agents of God's restorative work in all arenas of life.

PROJECT "VITALS"

Looking back at the scope and sequence for your project, please summarize the major details of your project (as tentatively planned) below.

"VITAL" STATISTIC	Total Number
Total # of instructional units involving service-learning	
Total # of learning activities/lessons	
Total # of service experiences	
Approximate # of days per week *(on which any aspect related to service-learning is addressed)*	
Approximate # of hours per week *(in which any aspect related to service-learning is addressed)*	

List below the <u>reflection methods</u> used in your project. (Provide a brief bulleted list, comprised of single words or short phrases—e.g., "Journals.")

-
-
-
-
-

List below the <u>assessment methods</u> used in your project. (Provide a brief bulleted list, comprised of single words or short phrases—e.g., "Group project.")

-
-
-
-
-

Briefly list below the lesson plans/activities in which students will have the opportunity to provide input into the project ("student voice") and/or assume leadership roles.

-
-
-
-
-

PROJECT EVALUATION PLANNING

Please review the project outcomes you identified earlier in this planning template, and then complete the questions below.

1. Restate/copy the major learning goals you identified for students below. For each, describe how you will know if the goal has been attained. *Please be as specific as possible as to how you will measure the achievement of the goals.*

2. Restate/copy the major service goals you identified for the community being served below. For each, describe how you will know if the goal has been attained. *Please be as specific as possible as to how you will measure the achievement of the goals.*

3. In each of the service-learning goals of Christian education that you linked to your project, please describe how for each you will know if the goal has been attained. *Please be as specific as possible as to how you will measure the achievement of the goals*, including: (a) promoting Christ-likeness in students; (b) helping students develop a biblical worldview; (c) teaching students how to be servant leaders; (d) helping students understand their role as lifelong agents of restoration in God's enduring story; and (e) other related goals.

4. Describe how you will know whether and how the project has helped students to develop personally, in terms of discovering and developing their unique talents and gifts. *Please be as specific as possible as to how you will measure the achievement of this goal.*

PROJECT LOGISTICS

There are many logistical considerations involved with planning the service components of a service-learning project. Complete the table below, and consider challenges, resources needed (e.g., financial, people), and strategies for addressing each.

Administrative Task	Challenges	Resources Needed	Strategies
Gaining administrator permission/ support			
Scheduling the service experiences			
Gaining parents' permission/ support			
Communicating with parents about the experience and how it connects to classroom			
Transportation			
Materials/ equipment			
Potential risks (including liability, insurance, injury, supervision of students, etc.)			

PROJECT BUDGET

Provide a proposed budget for the project. A total cost should be estimated, as well as itemized costs for each category. It is understood that this will involve estimates and that actual costs may differ; however, please base your estimate on research/inquiries you have done and your best effort to approximate the costs.

CATEGORY	DESCRIPTION OF ITEMS (please bullet/list by item)	ESTIMATED COST OF ITEMS (please bullet/list by item)
Class materials		
Materials for service experiences		
Transportation to and from service experiences		
"Wrapping up" costs, such as celebration events, publication/ presentation materials, etc. (if applicable)		
Other:		
TOTAL ESTIMATED COST for project	_____	$

REFLECTING ON YOUR PROPOSAL

1. In a few sentences, describe your biggest hopes for your project. What are you most excited about?

2. Briefly discuss how you will inspire your students to share your excitement.

3. In one or two sentences, please describe your biggest concerns about your project.

4. Briefly discuss one or two ways you can process through those concerns (e.g., what do you need to resolve them or to feel more confident about them?).

5. When you think about your project, what do you feel your strengths are (in your knowledge, skills, resources, etc.) to carry out the project successfully?

6. When you think about your project, what do you feel may be lacking (in your knowledge, skills, resources, etc.) or that you need more of, in order to carry out the project successfully?

7. What can you and others (e.g., school leaders) do to support you in regard to your answer for #6?

Next Steps

1. If you are a teacher, use the project planning template provided in this chapter to begin sketching out a service-learning project.

2. If you are a school leader, invite a small set of teachers to pilot a service-learning project in their course or grade. Share the project planning template provided in this chapter with them, and set target goals for when sections of the proposal should be completed. Meet regularly with teachers to track their progress and provide any support they need in designing their service-learning projects.

Questions for Discussion

1. Does the project planning template provided in this chapter show promise for planning for service-learning at our school? Why or why not? How might we use and/or adapt the template to our unique setting and faculty culture?

2. How can we structure the planning process for service-learning to ensure that viable projects are the result? How can we leverage professional development, collaborative work groups, release time, and accountability methods to this end?

3. How can we ensure age-appropriate student involvement in planning service-learning?

5
Supporting Service-Learning

In addition to a well-thought-out plan crafted by teachers (as described in the preceding chapter), service-learning requires extensive support from school leaders. Effective service-learning requires funding, logistical support, release time, collaboration, accountability, and—perhaps most importantly—professional development for faculty. This chapter outlines the need for each of these supports and offers suggestions for how school leaders can develop and provide them, thereby creating an environment that is conducive for service-learning.

Service-learning, whether implemented in one classroom or across an entire school, requires both innovative teachers *and* supportive school leaders. Besides the vision-casting and philosophical support that must come from school leadership, there is a very practical side to successful service-learning to which leaders must attend. This includes tasks like securing funding for projects, ensuring faculty have needed expertise and time for planning, and providing ongoing support while projects are being implemented. It is not enough for school leaders to simply give their "blessing" to service-learning; rather, teachers will need significant support across these and other areas for their projects to be successful.

This chapter explores some of the ways that school leaders can provide strategic and tactical support for service-learning in the classroom, through funding, logistical support, accountability mechanisms, release time, and professional development. We also discuss ways to pace the implementation of schoolwide service-learning, as well as how to transform schools' current service opportunities into a comprehensive and integrated approach to serving in the Christian school.

Funding for Service-Learning

Securing funding for projects is beyond the scope of responsibility that can be reasonably expected of teachers, unless they are given substantial discretionary funds each year for classroom use (which is relatively uncommon in any educational setting). Most likely, teachers will not have a large budget with which to work, and school leadership will need to plan ahead in the budget process to allocate sufficient funds for service-learning. Although we often get requests for "how much" should be budgeted for service-learning, we do not have a magic number as each school and project will be different. However, we do recommend that the annual school budget include a line item for service-learning, and that each class that is implementing service-learning be provided with a baseline allocation of funds. As the first year of implementation progresses and projects take shape, it is likely that some projects will cost more than originally allocated, and others will cost less. Allocation of funds can be reevaluated on an as-needed basis.

In addition to actual costs (i.e., transportation, project supplies and materials, etc.), school leaders should consider how they could incentivize teachers to become excited about developing their projects (as opposed to viewing service-learning as "one more thing" required by administration). For example, teachers who are in their first year of implementing service-learning can be given a small stipend on top of their base salary, in recognition of the unique demands of leading a service-learning project and rewarding the innovation for developing one. While all schools may not be in a position to offer a similar financial incentive, school leaders can identify other ways of showing appreciation for the work involved in implementing service-learning. Professional release time for planning (or to make up grading or class administration time) are all ways that administrators can help to lighten the load for teachers as they move toward a new pedagogy.

It's important to note that service-learning—as a project with high "public relations" value—is potentially fundable through private giving or grants. For example, we know of one school that applied for and received a few hundred dollars from the local newspaper toward a service-learning project, as part of the paper's initiative to recognize and sponsor community involvement among school students. Other area businesses are also potential sources of funding, especially if the requests are for projects that directly impact the local community. Consider approaching businesses as "sponsors," which is familiar terminology for small business owners who may already be accustomed to sponsoring sports teams or other youth activities. As a side benefit, approaching local businesses also helps to build further relationships between the school and the community.

Finally, the question of funding also raises the important topic of school board involvement and knowledge of service-learning, since the school board is likely the body that approves the annual budget for the school. In the context of asking for funding for service-learning, school leaders will need to present a strong case for the validity of service-learning and how it relates to the mission of the school. Once funding is granted and projects are underway, regular updates to the board on these projects are crucial, so that board members can see the impact on students and the community. A well-informed board is a board that will not only see the value of funding service-learning, but also help to champion the cause of service-learning to the broader school community and beyond.

Logistical Support

Providing logistical support is one of the most critical ways school leaders can support the implementation of service-learning. When we first talk with school leaders about the impact of service-learning on teachers, we often describe service-learning as a "yearlong field trip." We ask school leaders to describe how their faculty feel about managing scheduling, chaperones, permission slips, transportation money, liability forms, and the trip itself—and then multiply that times 180 days of instruction! This empathy-building exercise usually concludes with school leaders recognizing they need to find a way to offer administrative support to faculty engaged in service-learning.

That support needs to begin back in the planning stages, when faculty are developing their projects and beginning to think through the logistics of service-learning. Common needs include making phone calls to coordinate plans with service sites, arranging schedules, securing bus transportation for trips, purchasing supplies, and arranging substitute teacher coverage. Schools may need to shift some responsibilities of their office staff to free up time for someone to serve the needs of teachers as they plan and implement service-learning.

One school we know hired a part-time service-learning coordinator to provide administrative support to faculty who were planning projects. The coordinator's responsibilities included everything from figuring out transportation costs to filling out documents for the school's insurance carrier. In one instance, she even sat with two teachers who were nervous about reaching out to a community agency and coached them through the call. For faculty who are more used to focusing on pedagogy and curriculum, administrative support like this can help them jump over a myriad of logistical hurdles while planning. Making this support available during the planning process—such as while faculty are completing the sections of the template (in chapter 4) related to logistics and budgeting—can go a long way in ensuring not only that the template will be completed, but also that faculty will feel well-supported and confident in implementing the project.

Although not every school will be able to hire administrative support dedicated to service-learning, it's important to recognize that this support is crucial and must be identified and provided early in the process. Where funds do not exist for additional staff or if reshuffling current staff responsibilities is not possible, parent volunteers may be willing to help with administrative needs—especially if they are allowed to participate in the actual service-learning activities and can see the value of projects firsthand. This will become even more the case as service-learning is established as an important part of the school's culture and as parents, students, and staff alike come to see its value and benefits for students and the community. As excitement grows about service-learning, so too will the willingness of parents and other school community members to volunteer.

Regardless of how staffing is arranged, the specific logistical support that is needed by faculty (and their school leaders) often includes the following:

- Managing the master schedule for the school's service-learning initiative;
- Making contact with organizations outside of the school with whom service-learning partnerships will be developed;
- Arranging the logistics of service activities (scheduling, transportation, waivers and other paperwork, confirmations, supplies, etc.);
- Managing the budget for service-learning projects;
- Maintaining detailed and comprehensive records documenting service-learning activities; and
- Assisting classroom teachers in completing paperwork, including providing reminders and accountability for deadlines.

Service-Learning Snapshot:
When one school attempted to appoint a service-learning coordinator from within the ranks of current faculty and staff, they found that no one had the time available to take over the role. So, the administration looked outside of regular employees to find a school parent who might be interested. They ended up finding a school parent who had previously worked in a local outreach ministry, and was looking for very limited part-time work. She was excited about the opportunity to use her gifts and talents on a part-time basis, which also allowed her to join her children on their service-learning trips. Working only between five and eight hours per week—and many of those hours from home—the part-time service-learning coordinator was able to support the efforts of classroom teachers. One of the most helpful ways she did so was in making calls and arranging visits to service sites. Without this kind of logistical support, many of the projects planned by teachers might have floundered in the "idea" stage and never come to fruition.

Accountability Mechanisms

We've noticed that—just like their students—most school leaders and faculty will miss deadlines if they fail to break down assignments into small chunks and receive regular reminders of due dates. In fact, most adults in the school building function very well with the educational accountability "tactics" we use with students, such as writing due dates in our planners, producing multiple drafts of work on a schedule, and receiving emails that remind us about assignments. The corollaries for service-learning planning include things like deadlines for completing sections of the template (in chapter 4) and allowing for drafting and resubmission of sections. In addition, it's helpful to develop an overall timeline for completion of the template, and then create a parallel timeline with strategies (such as reminder emails and check-in meetings) to assist teachers in meeting deadlines.

Another accountability strategy is to develop quarterly online surveys or forms (see the sample "Service-Learning Progress Report" provided in chapter 7) that can be emailed to faculty, with a one-week deadline for completion. These touch points are helpful for keeping the service-learning planning process at the forefront of teachers' minds. Moreover, they present an opportunity for gathering data on where faculty are in the process, what questions are emerging, and what additional support they may need in the planning process. This information can be valuable for monitoring and adjusting the planning process as time progresses.

Release Time

The time and effort needed during the planning stage for service-learning can put additional stress on the schedule of an already busy teacher. As much as possible, we highly recommend providing professional release time for teachers so that they can plan and even collaborate with other service-learning teachers during the course of a normal school day. Even with dedicated professional development sessions and supportive working groups, we have found that faculty may still need additional "time on task" that cannot be found during the regular work day. As a side benefit of providing release time, teachers tend to feel valued and affirmed—and the importance of service-learning is strongly emphasized when school leaders are willing to call in a substitute teacher to cover classes while teachers plan.

> *Service-Learning Snapshot:*
> *One school implementing service-learning had a part-time coordinator, whose teaching load as a faculty member brought her to full-time status. This individual helped to provide appropriate accountability for the teachers as they planned and implemented their projects, by meeting with them for monthly check-ins and support. Though she had no supervisory authority, the fact that teachers were scheduled to meet regularly with her helped motivate teachers to keep their projects moving ahead.*

Of course, there will be limited resources for release time and substitutes at any school, and it will be key to budget wisely for this option. However, using a portion of existing funds or allocating future funds for service-learning planning can yield an excellent return on investment. This is especially the case when effective accountability methods are put into place, as described above.

Professional Development

Almost all Christian schools have ongoing professional development (PD) opportunities for faculty, whether entire days when school is not in session or late-start PD. Research shows that faculty find PD experiences more effective when they are "coherent" with—or closely tied to—the overall instructional objectives of the school (Swaner 2016, 25). If service-learning is a major instructional initiative of the school, it makes sense to dedicate ongoing PD opportunities to planning for service-learning. This also demonstrates to faculty the importance of service-learning: if the school is willing to devote multiple PD hours to it, service-learning must be something that matters to the instructional culture of the school.

The planning template presented in chapter 4 can be easily adapted for use in PD days or sessions. Since each of the sections of the template builds on the preceding section, it can be broken up over a series of PD experiences, whether on a separate day or session. For example, project outcomes must be identified before mapping out the scope and sequence of service-learning; these two tasks can be separated into different PD experiences, and scheduled one after the other. Harnessing existing PD for service-learning planning in this way greatly reduces the need to identify additional time for faculty to work on planning, whether during or outside of the school day.

Further, devoting PD time and resources to service-learning creates space for faculty to collaborate on planning their projects. This is important since another hallmark of effective PD experiences is "collective participation" (Swaner 2016, 27), or PD opportunities where faculty are able to collaborate with their colleagues. As discussed in an earlier chapter, we have seen that service-learning planning is more effective when faculty are able to come together on a regular basis to work on their plans. Pairing or teaming small groups of faculty encourages sharing of ideas, peer support, and mutual accountability for deadlines. This is true not only during the planning phase, but also throughout implementation of service-learning. Collaborative work groups can meet during PD sessions, common planning periods, or other mutually convenient times.

Grouping faculty by grade level or common subject area is a natural way of creating these kinds of groups. For example, all second-grade teachers can collaborate on service-learning planning for that grade level, as could an entire high school science department. These groups can work together on drafting sections of the project template, engaging in constructive questioning and feedback, and eventually in supporting each other through project implementation. One potential by-product of such a collaborative working group is increased horizontal or vertical alignment (in the case of grade-level and subject-matter grouping, respectively) of both content and service experiences. This is clearly a benefit for teaching and learning at the school, even outside of service-learning projects—demonstrating yet again how service-learning can be a powerful pedagogy for transforming instructional culture.

Service-Learning Case Story: Harnessing PD to Build Service-Learning Capacity

Working together with or alongside of colleagues who are also planning service-learning projects is an ideal venue in which to foster professional learning communities (PLCs). One school used a PLC model to roll out service-learning incrementally. Faculty were divided into three equal cohorts, with each cohort spending a planning year followed by an implementation year (so Cohort A planned in Year One and implemented in Year Two, Cohort B planned in Year Two and implemented in Year Three, and Cohort C planned in Year Three and implemented in Year Four).

Each cohort functioned as a mini-PLC through its planning and evaluation years. Teachers in the planning year were oriented to service-learning through a half-day workshop, which was held during the PD days prior to the start of the school year. Teachers were also given two half-days of release time in the fall to work on their project proposals. This work session was a critical part of the overall support that the school provided to the teachers, as they did not have to create their proposals on their own time after school or during prep periods.

During these work sessions, school leaders were present the entire time to listen to the emerging plans and to ask coaching questions to help the teachers refine their thoughts and solidify their initial plans. Also, the school's service-learning coordinator was present and available for consultation. Teachers were able to collaborate with one another and receive feedback on their ideas from peers. A debriefing time was held at the end, which incorporated a reflection exercise to help teachers process their experience. School leaders built in reflection into every PD experience as a way to model the importance of reflection in teachers' own service-learning projects.

Then throughout the year, each teacher met monthly with the service-learning coordinator, who provided ongoing consultation as well as reflection and reporting activities. A second day in the spring (again providing release time to teachers) mimicked that of the fall. Finally, teachers were allowed to utilize another half-day of release time during the spring to work independently on their projects, at their discretion.

Come the fall, the teachers in this school reported feeling prepared to implement their projects, given the time they had invested through PD the preceding year. Perhaps most importantly, teachers were highly invested in—and felt a strong sense of ownership for—their projects. This translated into their willingness to meet with and informally mentor the next cohort involved in planning, to share insights and learning with them. Ultimately, the process contributed to a greater sense of teacher involvement and overall collegiality in the school's instructional culture.

Pacing Implementation

When school leaders decide to implement service-learning in a significant way—i.e., across multiple grade levels and disciplines—an important question that needs to be answered is how to roll out service-learning. We have found that the rate of the roll-out largely depends on the preparedness of faculty to engage in service-learning, the size of the school, and the resources (financial and personnel) available to sustain service-learning initiatives.

Regardless of the rate of roll-out, we recommend that any school that is new to service-learning begin with a limited number of projects as pilots. Pilot projects enable school leaders and teachers alike to learn firsthand what makes for a successful service-learning project, and what pitfalls to avoid. Particularly for larger schools with sizeable faculty, we also recommend considering a "wave" approach to rolling out service learning. This means having several grades or courses start a service-learning project each year, so that it takes multiple years (often three to five) to get the entire school up and running with service-learning. The benefits of a graduated implementation of service-learning are many, and include:

- Building momentum for service-learning, which expands upon successes year after year (especially if "early adopters" are among the first to pilot and plan projects, and then can serve as "advocates" for the pedagogy for other faculty that may be more reluctant or skeptical);

- The ability to conduct professional development with a segment of the faculty as opposed to all at the same time, which allows for *depth* in activities as opposed to *breadth* (with the former being more important to launching a complex project like service-learning);
- Possibilities for peer support and mentoring, both among teachers planning and implementing at the same time, and between teachers who have already initiated service-learning projects and those who are just beginning;
- Opportunities for ongoing improvement and refinement of the service-learning process and total program at the school with each year of implementation; and
- Gradual, incremental increases in the school's budget commitment to service-learning, which allows for demonstration of success to stakeholders (i.e., the school board, parents) and prospective funders.

For these reasons, schools that are just beginning service-learning—and those that have experimented in the past, but are considering scaling up their efforts—should consider how they can support their faculty and staff through an intentional and thoughtful roll-out process.

Moving Toward a Comprehensive and Integrated Approach to Serving

Many Christian schools recognize the importance of serving for students. In fact, we would be hard-pressed to find a Christian school where some kind of service was not occurring, whether through a community service requirement, one-time outreaches, ongoing campaigns or "drives," peer-to-peer service, or mission trips. When school leaders and teachers first begin thinking about service-learning, they often question the value of current service opportunities that are at the school and whether or how they might "transform" their efforts into more robust service-learning.

Although we hope this book presents a compelling case for service-learning, we do not at all mean to discount the other forms of service in which Christian school students and teachers engage. Many of these forms are valuable and rewarding for students. However, we find the following two questions to be helpful for school leaders and teachers who wish to weigh the value of their current service opportunities, in light of the potential power of service-learning:

1. Are the service opportunities offered by the school also available to students in other settings, such as their churches, youth groups, or families? (Food and clothing drives are good examples of fairly universal service activities.) If so, it may be worth asking the question of how the school can offer service experiences that students can't get elsewhere. Another way to state this is as follows: how can the school setting be harnessed to create unique and powerful service opportunities for students?

2. Is there a meaningful connection between current service opportunities at the school and the "real work" of learning in the classroom? If not, students will likely do some good for others, and they may even learn something along the way—but overall, the impact of service that is disconnected from learning is limited, both for the one doing the serving and the ones being served.

To help answer these questions, we recommend that school

leaders conduct an audit of service opportunities at the school (which was a "Next Step" suggested in an earlier chapter). Once this is completed, leaders can step back and assess their school's service "portfolio" for depth, intentionality, and impact.

To help in this self-examination process, we've developed a continuum that describes the range of orientations to service we've identified in Christian schools (below).

On one extreme of this continuum is the "slog and log" approach—where students are required to engage in service for the "sake" of doing service, simply because it's the "right" thing to do as Christians (and as a Christian school). Typically, service opportunities that fall at this end of the continuum have little to no connection with learning and spiritual formation at the school. As noted on the continuum, we tend to find that community service hour requirements and "one-off" service events tend toward the "slog and log" orientation.

By way of contrast, service at the opposite side of the continuum can be characterized as being motivated by "who we are" in Christ. By this we mean that service is an integral part of students' identity in Christ—as those who engage in service as a response to Him and His work—as well as in the identity of the Christian school itself, as a community of believers who are engaged in God's restorative work.

In contrast to the "slog and log" approach, we find that service at the "who we are" end of the continuum tends to be more closely tied to the school's mission (both in terms of academics and spiritual formation) and to be more integrated throughout its core programs. Courses that involve outreach—and of course, service-learning programs—tend toward to the "who we are" side.

A good question for school leaders to ask, after conducting an audit of their school's service opportunities, is to assess their overall "portfolio." Does the bulk of service happening at the school tend toward one side of this continuum, or does the school have a "balanced" portfolio? Is the school interested in moving their service opportunities more toward the "who we are" side of the continuum?

If the answer to this last question is "yes," there are several options available to a school. The first is to eliminate the bulk of lower-impact service outright, being careful to explain to all school stakeholders that the school is not moving away from service itself, but instead is moving towards more *meaningful* service. If a service opportunity is a cherished tradition in the school, special care will need to be taken in internal marketing to ensure that people understand why it is going away, and how much more impactful service-learning will be. Particularly in the case of a community service requirement, service-learning is often welcomed because it brings the service experiences into the actual school day and calendar (thereby eliminating the necessity of students and families scrambling to devote hours outside of the school day). Most parents find this change appealing, given the busy schedule of today's families.

Service-Learning Snapshot:
After a year of evaluating their community service requirement, one school decided to abruptly do away with it in the first year they began implementing service-learning. In doing so, they were concerned about people's perception that the school was abandoning a long-standing program. However, there was no push-back at all, and the transition to service-learning was seamless—helped along by communication with families regarding the reasons for the change, and how the change would help their students to engage in more meaningful service as part of their academic coursework.

Another strategy is to phase out other activities as service-learning is gradually phased in. In situations where graduation requirements must be changed, this is a common approach. For instance, if a school has a community service requirement for their high school, they can target a specific class for which the requirement would no longer be in force. In such a case, it would be logical to target the lower grades (such as the current ninth and tenth grades) to be released from the old service requirement. These two grades could then begin implementing service-learning projects—in essence, "swapping" service-learning for the service requirement. Grades eleven and twelve would continue the program (in which they have likely already invested significant hours) until graduation, so that within two years, the community service requirement would be eliminated and all four high school grades could be engaged in service-learning.

A final question is exactly how integrated and widespread service-learning ought to be at a school. Certainly, offering a service-learning experience in every grade level is one approach, but a number of schools have paired grade levels to work on a single project, or engaged an entire academic department in service-learning across all grades. Particularly for a smaller school with fewer faculty members, these types of approaches may be a good option. For example, middle school grades (sixth through eighth) might work together in their science classes to develop a hydroponics lab or school garden, and donate the food they grow to a local food pantry. Or eleventh- and twelfth-grade English classes could partner together to work with a senior citizen center to interview seniors about their lives for publication on a website. While keeping students engaged over multiple years with the same project may be challenging, it can also present an opportunity for students to practice leadership skills as they are given increasing responsibility as they advance in grades. This is important because leadership skills are often part of the "hidden curriculum" of service-learning, and servant leadership is an important standard for service-learning in Christian schools (see chapter 3).

Ultimately, no two schools have the exact same profile when it comes to how they integrate service-learning into their programs. Some schools may be able to shift gears without any questions asked. Others may need a multiyear approach to give stakeholders time to see the power of service-learning and how it can eclipse other service efforts in scope and impact. Each school leadership team will need to examine its own programs and school culture to discern if and how to move away from any existing service opportunities, thereby making way for more engaged and meaningful service.

Service-Learning Case Story: Adopting a Nursing Home to Show God's Love

A second-grade teacher decided to anchor the service-learning project in the Bible curriculum for the year, which focused on "loving others as Jesus loves us." The teacher felt that students were at a developmentally ideal age to both memorize Scripture and begin to "live it out." For example, memory verses each month focused on God's love, Jesus' service to others, and the Bible's instruction to care for others. Service-learning opportunities offered students the chance to put these verses into action, by learning how to love others through service. In addition, the second-grade teacher decided to partner with the art teacher to utilize the class's art projects for service-learning. The broad outcomes the teacher identified for service-learning were students':

- Memorization of Bible verses related to God's love;
- Ability to apply these verses in an understanding of how they were called to love others, just as Jesus loved them;
- Ability to show God's love through tangible gifts and interaction with nursing home residents;
- Developing writing skills through journaling; and
- Mastery of second-grade art concepts through the production of cards and crafts.

Given the young age of the students, the second-grade teacher thought carefully about service opportunities that would be age-appropriate and not overly challenging or uncomfortable for students. The teacher discussed various options with the elementary principal, and landed upon the idea of adopting a local nursing home. The elementary school had sporadically sent classes to visit the nursing home in the past (for example, to sing carols right before Christmas break). Both the teacher and the principal agreed it was a welcoming and age-appropriate setting where the school had already made inroads for service.

The teacher decided that the class would do approximately one project a month geared toward service-learning, which the class worked on during Bible and art classes. The projects were seasonal or holiday-themed in nature. In addition, four trips to the nursing home were also made, with parents invited to chaperone and join the trips. On each trip students had opportunity to interact directly with residents and provide them with a craft or project they had developed, and/or perform a song or mini-play. The teacher used the first month of school to orient students and families to the concept of service-learning, and then developed the schedule for the rest of the year as follows:

Month	Bible Concept	Theme/Holiday	Activity	Service Trip
October	God shows us love by caring for creation (Leviticus 26:4).	Harvest	Apple and pumpkin cutout cards, mailed to nursing home	n/a
November	We can give thanks because God's love endures forever (Psalm 118:1).	Thanksgiving	Making cornucopias with real fruit	Trip to nursing home to deliver cornucopias
December	God so loved us that He sent His only son (John 3:16).	Christmas	Making Christmas ornaments	Trip to nursing home to deliver ornaments and to carol
January	n/a	n/a	n/a	n/a
February	God is love (1 John 4:8b).	Valentine's Day	Making Valentine's Day cutout cards	Trip to nursing home to deliver cards
March	It's not luck! God showers us with His grace (John 1:16).	St. Patrick's Day	Making Scripture door hangers; mailed to nursing home	n/a
April	God showed His love for us by dying for us (Romans 5:8).	Easter	Stained glass cross craft; practicing an Easter mini-play (presentation of the gospel)	Trip to nursing home to deliver Easter cards and perform mini-play
May	God cares for the flowers, and look how He cares for us (Matthew 6:28–30)!	May Brings Spring Flowers	Pressed flower bouquet thank-you cards; delivered to residents by school staff to say thank you for the year	

The main reflection activity implemented by the teacher was journaling. After each activity and service trip, the students worked on a journal that described their experience and how it related to the Bible content and verse being studied that month. Students shared their journals with each other as well as worked on them at home. Journals contained both a written portion and a space for students to draw a picture of their experience serving. The teacher spent significant time in class debriefing students' learning and discussing responses in their journals.

Service-learning portfolios were used to assess students' learning. These portfolios contained photographs of students' work for each month, copies of students' journal entries, students' printed writing of the memory verse for each unit, and the sticker chart used throughout the year to mark off students' Bible verse memorization progress. Portfolios were shared at parent-teacher conferences and sent home at the end of the year. In addition, pictures of students' work and of the class serving were displayed at school concerts, on the school's social media sites, and in the school newsletter.

Next Steps

1. Once again, review the audit of service opportunities that you generated at the end of the introductory chapter. Determine the percentage of opportunities that fall into the "slog and log" category, and what percentage move the school and its students toward a "who we are" approach to service.

2. Write a draft mission statement for service at your school, that imagines service opportunities as being intentionally tied to your school's larger mission and integrated into the curriculum. Use this mission statement to jumpstart conversations about deepening students' learning through service at the school.

Discussion Questions:

1. How open to innovation in teaching and learning is our school culture?

2. What kind of practical support do teachers in our school need in order to effectively implement service-learning?

3. How can we leverage the professional development events already on our school calendar for preparing service-learning?

4. What practical obstacles to service-learning exist in our school? How can we work to overcome those obstacles?

5. Does our school have service opportunities, such as a community service program, that could be transformed into a service-learning initiative? If so, what steps would we need to take to make that change?

6
Assessing Service-Learning

Service-learning necessitates a significant investment of resources on the part of a school and its faculty, leaders, students, and community partners. In order to ensure those resources are being invested and stewarded wisely, it's crucial to assess whether service-learning is having a significant and positive impact on student learning and development, as well as community needs. From identifying outcomes, to choosing instruments, to analyzing data, determining the impact of service-learning requires a robust assessment plan. This chapter presents a systematic approach for assessing service-learning and provides practical guidance for measuring the diverse and complex outcomes of service-learning.

Not surprisingly, figuring out whether service-learning is successful is much more difficult than determining whether third graders have mastered multiplication tables. An important question, though, is why is it different? The answer to this question can provide valuable insight and direction for how to go about assessing the impact of service-learning experiences. Just as service-learning is a different pedagogy from much of what happens instructionally in K–12 Christian education, the way it is assessed also needs to be different. Service-learning assessment is fundamentally different for at least three reasons, as depicted in the table below.

Assessment Dimensions of Service-Learning

Assessment Dimension	Service-Learning
Outcomes	Multivariate (cognitive, social, affective, physical, spiritual)
Learning Sites	Classroom, community, home
Constituents	Students, teacher, community members (being served), community partner(s) and organizations

First, service-learning bundles together different outcomes from *multiple domains*. Service-learning outcomes include cognition (i.e., mastery of course content) but also extend to social, affective, physical, and spiritual outcomes. For example, we might hope that students who participate in service-learning would learn how to work together as a team, to be able to interact with community members, to develop empathy for those they serve, and to understand they are the "hands and feet of Jesus" when they serve others. Further, as discussed in earlier chapters, service-learning is a pedagogy that helps students to grow in Christ-likeness, servant leadership, biblical worldview, and their unique God-given talents and abilities, among other domains. With all of these outcomes in view, we can say that service-learning assessment must be multivariate in nature.

In addition to these multiple domains, service-learning also encompasses *multiple sites* for learning. Service-learning directly involves students in the classroom, various places in the community, and in their homes (particularly if the school engages families in supporting service-learning). In order to understand the full impact of service-learning, it's important to understand the learning that happens in each of these sites—and perhaps more importantly, how students make connections between them (as discussed in chapter 1, those connections are often mediated by intentional and structured reflection).

Moreover, rather than just interacting with their teachers, classmates, and parents, students in service-learning experiences are working with community members, local civic leaders, church or ministry leaders, and so forth. Service-learning can (and ought to) have an impact on all those involved with service-learning, both in the school and the community. Thus, assessment needs to take into account the multiple constituents involved in service-learning, as well as the ways in which their interaction impacts the outcomes of service-learning.

All this is to say that assessing the outcomes of service-learning is a complicated task, and as such, we can't expect that a single test or statistic can provide a full picture of the impact of service-learning. However, just because assessing service-learning is a complex process doesn't mean that it can't be done well. A robust approach to assessment can determine whether and how service-learning is having a significant and positive impact on student learning and development, for the school as a whole, and on meeting community needs. Such an assessment approach attends to the "various parts of the service-learning experience, to get a full view of the learning journey" (Farber 2011, 49). The rest of this chapter will lay out a framework for assessing service-learning, as well as specific approaches and strategies that we have found to be helpful in our work with schools.

A Framework for Assessing Service-Learning

A framework for assessing service-learning consists of two components. The first is the range of areas in which the effects of service-learning should be measured. In our work with schools, educators have typically identified three levels of assessment that are of interest: (1) student learning and development; (2) school improvement; and (3) community impact. Each of these areas may be of more interest to a certain constituency than others—for example, school improvement may be particularly important to school leaders and board members—but all three are key for understanding the full impact of service-learning.

The second component is the assessment process itself, which we have broken down into five specific steps: (1) identifying outcomes; (2) choosing assessment measures; (3) collecting data (baseline, formative, and summative); (4) analyzing data; and (5) using the results to make adjustments. To help provide a visual for this full scope of service-learning assessment, we've developed a service-learning assessment matrix, which can help in building an assessment plan.

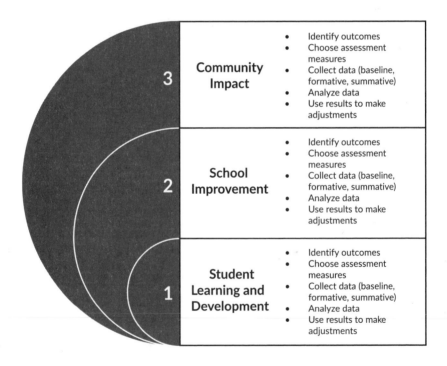

As depicted above, some areas of assessment are "nestled" within others; for example, student learning and development is nestled within school improvement and community impact, and school improvement in turn is nestled within community impact. The idea is that the impact on students will in turn affect the school and the community, and changes at the school will necessarily impact the larger community. Change in any one level is interrelated with change in the other two. While the assessment steps look fairly similar across the three areas, there are some important distinctions and approaches that we will point out as we review each in the remainder of this chapter.

First, however, we want to point out that this chapter has been written with schoolwide service-learning initiatives that connect to broad school outcomes and improvement initiatives in mind. As such, teams of school leaders, teachers, and community partners may be most interested in the model we offer here. However, we know that this guidebook may be used by an individual teacher in just one classroom. If the teacher is conducting service-learning in isolation, it may be tempting to skip the assessment piece. However, even in that case, the basic principles we've outlined here can apply; while an individual teacher's assessment plan will obviously be less comprehensive than a schoolwide plan, it can still yield valuable information about the success of service-learning. We are strong proponents of the concept that all pedagogy should be assessed to determine the attainment of outcomes, including in a single classroom. So, whether an entire school is implementing service-learning, or one grade-level teacher is embarking on a solo journey to discover the impact of service-learning, assessment is key.

Identifying Outcomes
As mentioned in earlier chapters, identifying outcomes at the beginning of the service-learning process is essential

for developing projects themselves. Outcomes serve a dual purpose, though, in that they can be used as yardsticks by which to measure the impact of service-learning. For this reason, assessment planning should begin by identifying the outcomes to be assessed in the three areas identified for service-learning impact—student learning and development, school improvement, and community impact.

> **Service-Learning Snapshot:**
> A middle school teacher decided to engage the class in a project that involved serving at a local base for missionaries on furlough, tied to course content on global cultures. For the project, students spent service hours cleaning and doing repairs at the base as well as learning from missionaries about their experiences (through both formal interviews and relationship-building). To identify outcomes for service-learning, the teacher drew upon those in the curriculum guide for the class related to appreciating other cultures, recognizing the diversity of God's creation through various people groups, and understanding the challenges in particular faced by developing countries. In addition, the teacher identified outcomes that were unique to the service-learning project, such as listening for understanding, serving others, and meeting their needs with humility. The principal at the school linked student learning for the project to schoolwide expected student outcomes, including developing servanthood and practicing cross-cultural skills. From all of these sources, a comprehensive list of diverse outcomes was developed for the service-learning experience.

In terms of *student learning and development*, outcomes are the concepts, dispositions, or skills that students ought to know, be, or be able to do as a result of a given educational experience. To identify key outcomes targeted by service-learning, teachers should examine the objectives of their courses, and school leaders should look to the curriculum as well as to schoolwide expected student outcomes (which, ideally, all schools should develop). As discussed earlier, student outcomes from service-learning are typically multidimensional in nature. They can relate directly to course content or to knowledge gained from service itself. They can also include abilities like reflection, self-assessment, leadership, and teamwork. Outcomes can also be identified in the areas of spiritual formation, biblical worldview development, personal growth, self-discovery, and disposition toward serving others—to name a few.

Outcomes related to the second area of service-learning impact—*school improvement*—should also be identified. This is important in order to link service-learning to the instructional "heart" of the school, as opposed to making service-learning just an "add-on" to the curriculum. Good sources for outcomes can include the school's strategic plan, continuous school improvement plan, curricular review process, and professional development goals. For accredited schools, service-learning outcomes can be connected to accreditation standards and/or major recommendations from visiting teams.

It is also important to point back to the standards for service-learning that were identified in chapter 3 when considering service-learning outcomes. By incorporating standards into targeted outcomes, educators will increase their chances of those standards being considered in project design and implementation. Ultimately, assessing school improvement outcomes drawn from these sources will enable leaders to paint a picture of how service-learning has impacted the overall school culture. This will help to answer the inevitable question from teachers, students, parents, and board members: is service-learning "worth it"?

Finally, in terms of *community impact*, community partners should be involved directly in determining the desired outcomes. Too often this is a "miss" when it comes to service-

Service-Learning Snapshot:
A fourth-grade class's service-learning project (in math) included making several trips throughout the year to a local rescue mission to assist in their distribution outreaches. Naturally, a significant number of chaperones were needed, and parents of students in the class gladly volunteered. While not a primary expected outcome of the project, one of the major benefits of this project was that parents—who had never been on a distribution line—were powerfully impacted by serving alongside their children. The school was able to document this impact by tracking comments on an annual parent survey, as well as a parent focus group that was conducted by the school's strategic planning committee. Data indicated the connections parents made on the trips and the experience of serving others deepened their commitment to the school. Ultimately, they became even more outspoken ambassadors for the school among their own friends and in their own neighborhoods, as they experienced the school's tangible impact on themselves, their children, and the broader community.

learning: educators imagine what community partners need and want, and set about to develop a project that they think addresses these needs and wants. They fail, however, to involve community partners in first identifying what service activities would be most useful to them, as well as what benefit the partners would like to see as a result of the project. This does not promote a good relationship with community partners, and can limit the overall effectiveness of the project and authenticity of the service in meeting a real need.

To prevent this scenario, educators should discuss desired community outcomes up-front with partners. In fact, this discussion should even precede conversations about logistics (e.g., when and how often students can visit the site, what students will be doing). It's easy to gloss over outcomes in favor of getting to specifics of what the project will look like, but this initial conversation will both build the relationship with the partner and provide language around desired outcomes relative to community impact. Some helpful questions to ask the community partner that can ultimately lead to specific, measurable outcomes are:

- Why are you interested in having our students come and serve?
- Ideally, what impact do you hope the students will have?
- What are the top three specific things you hope the students will accomplish while they are here?
- What benefit will this project be to you (and/or to those your organization serves)?
- How will you know if this project was a success or not? What evidence would you accept to know whether it has been successful?

An initial list of outcomes relative to community impact can be developed from these questions, which should then be vetted by the community partner with opportunity for input. Assuming all parties are in agreement, this list of outcomes can provide the basis for assessing community impact. It is possible that getting to an agreed-upon list may require some negotiation (especially to ensure that the outcomes are reasonable and attainable, and not too broad or too narrow). Rather than perceiving this as a negative, the negotiation process should be viewed as a healthy way to build relationships, refine expectations, clarify assumptions, and set boundaries for the service-learning experience—all of which can only benefit the school-partner relationship over the life of the project.

Choosing Assessment Measures

Once a comprehensive list of outcomes has been developed for each of the three areas of measurement—student learning and development, school improvement, and community impact—instruments need to be selected to assess the attainment of those outcomes. It's helpful to remember at the outset of this step that, again, service-learning is a complex pedagogy with multiple and diverse outcomes. A general principle of assessment to remember is that "the complexity of the data collection methods should roughly match the complexity of the phenomenon under investigation" (Swaner 2016a, 213). In practice, this means that a single assessment—such as standardized testing—will be insufficient to measure the full spectrum of service-learning outcomes.

One of the best ways to ensure that assessment is sufficiently complex is to utilize a "mixed-methods" approach, whether examining student learning and development, community impact, or school improvement. This means using both qualitative and quantitative measures. For example, student outcomes can be assessed via unit and course grades (quantitative measures), as well as portfolios of student work, journals, and group projects (qualitative measures). School improvement assessment can include changes in institutional data (such as retention and graduation rates) or parent surveys (all quantitative), as well as focus groups of school constituencies and student exit interviews (all qualitative). Community impact assessment can involve surveys of those served (quantitative) as well as interviews of community partners (qualitative).

We have often encountered school leaders and teachers who struggle with identifying the ways they can measure the outcomes of service-learning. Below is a sample list of both quantitative and qualitative instruments and approaches that are commonly used to assess service-learning, and with which we ourselves have had success in assessing project impact.

Ways to Measure Service-Learning Outcomes

QUANTITATIVE	QUALITATIVE

• Surveys (of parents, teachers, students, community members)
• Tests (classroom, standardized achievement, SAT/ACT)
• Course grades and GPA
• Institutional data (graduation rates, college attendance data, course selection data)
• Normed assessments (worldview, behavior, affect, beliefs, etc.)
• Participation or usage data (e.g., events, services offered)
• Community data/ statistics
	• Student work products (with rubrics for grading/ assessment):
	  • Journals
	  • Portfolios
	  • Group projects
	  • Papers or essays
	• Interviews (of parents, teachers, students, community members)
	• Focus groups (with parents, teachers, students, community members)
	• Service-learning products (e.g., school-community report, artifacts from service)

As you review this list of assessments, it's important to note that cherry-picking from both sides (quantitative and qualitative) isn't the same thing as achieving a mixed-methods approach. Rather, instruments should be carefully chosen for their potential to measure the specific outcomes of the service-learning project or projects.

From our experiences with assessing service-learning, we've identified some guiding principles for choosing outcome-appropriate measures. First, it's important to balance the use of "*distal*" and "*proximal*" measures. Distal measures are those which are *far removed from* the actual learning or serving experience, such as standardized tests (which are removed both in terms of time and service-learning content). Proximal measures are *close to* the learning or serving experience, such as unit tests or projects (again, both in terms of time and specificity to content). By way of illustration, a distal measure is akin to a doctor taking your temperature; it's easy to confirm that you have a fever, but impossible to tell why you have one. A proximal measure is more like the doctor using an otoscope to see whether or not you have an ear infection, so that more specific information about the root cause and extent of the infection can be obtained. It's important to note that most doctor visits involve *both* kinds of measures, and for good reason: both distal and proximal measures can help confirm—and then deepen—one's understanding. The same is true for assessing service-learning experiences.

Next, in planning service-learning assessment, it's important to remember that choices need to be made regarding the *level of measurement*. By this, we mean essentially the individuals or groups who will be the targets of assessment. Three such levels that are often targeted in classrooms and schools:

1. *Individual students* or classes can be tracked to show growth year over year. For example, all the students who are third graders today can be assessed next year when they are fourth graders. This can be helpful to show growth in students, but it can be difficult to parse out the normal effects of maturation versus the effects of service-learning. Comparing multiple years of data prior to the implementation service-learning can help to identify what "normal" growth looks like from one year to the next, which can be compared with data from service-learning implementation to tell whether there appears to be a

"boost" from the addition of the program.

2. On a second level, *whole classes or grades* can be compared with each other. For example, the performance of this year's sophomore class can be compared with last year's sophomore class. To determine whether this data is valid, however, it will be important to establish whether the two grades are "equivalent" in terms of demographics, learning ability, and so forth. To do this, it's best to create a profile of each class or grade, and compare the grades to determine the degree of equivalency.

3. Finally, in terms of the *whole school*, data can be compared with the school's past performance and/or with the performance of other schools (where normed samples are available).

Assessment within the community can follow a similar track (individual person or agency served, year-over-year differences, and comparison with other communities or similar populations).

Another assessment principle is to *avoid settling for convenience, but do aim for feasibility*. It's important to not just pick the "easiest" route when it comes to assessment, as that rarely leads to useful data to gauge the impact of service-learning properly. However, while convenience is not the goal, *feasibility* is. Instruments and the assessment process overall have to be doable given the school's existing resources (which includes people's time, school calendar, and budget—especially as some types of assessments cost money to administer and/or score). Similarly, it's key to avoid developing an assessment plan that "ate the school" or becomes the "one assessment plan to rule them all." While service-learning should be central to the instructional mission of the school, there are other important things that school leaders and teachers will want to know and assess (e.g., the effectiveness of the new elementary math curriculum or parents' perceptions of changes to the school's athletic program). Service-learning should certainly be a priority, but for obvious reasons it can't encompass everything that the school is doing and assessing. (In fact, it's our hope that the assessment principles offered in this chapter will prove helpful for readers as they think about assessment in all areas, and not just service-learning).

Finally, when planning assessment for service-learning, schools will need to *identify resources* needed for assessment. Christian education (and indeed all education) has become more data-driven than ever, which likely means that more school leaders and teachers are comfortable with understanding and using varied assessments. Even so, leading a school or teaching full-time doesn't often leave a lot of extra mental energy or hours to devote to designing an assessment plan for service-learning from scratch. Thus, it's a good idea to ask what resources are available to assist with assessment. Resources like online survey sites, consultants, faculty at Christian or other colleges, and other schools engaged in service-learning may prove helpful. We encourage readers to also to refer to chapter 7 of this book, which points to potentially useful resources.

Once assessment instruments have been selected for a project, the best way to plot out how they will be used is by developing a visual table, or map, that lists: (1) the area to be assessed (student learning and development, community impact, or school improvement); (2) the specific outcome to be assessed; and (3) the resources required and responsible party. To help visualize this, we've provided a small slice of an assessment map (with an example for three outcomes, in the area of assessing student learning) below.

Sample Assessment Table

Area	Outcome	Instrumentation	Responsible Party/Resources
Student Learning	Increased knowledge of course content	• Unit tests	• Classroom teacher; online student information system
		• Standardized testing	• Principal; standardized testing online results portal
Student Learning	Ability to apply course content to real-world situations	• Structured journals	• Classroom teacher; online platform for journal writing and submission
		• Culminating group presentation to community partner	• Classroom teacher, working with community partner to assess group presentations
Student Learning	Increased sense of God-given, unique abilities, and how to use those through service to others	• Structured journals	• Classroom teacher; online platform for journal writing and submission
		• Student exit interviews	• Service-learning coordinator; structured interview questions to be developed by service-learning team

In this sample, a variety of measures are used (both quantitative and qualitative) across all of the outcomes for student learning. When fleshed out to include all of the targeted areas of assessment (student learning and development, school improvement, and community impact) and related outcomes, the table would serve as a useful roadmap for how the teacher and school will conduct assessment for the project.

Collecting Data

After instruments are selected, the next step is to collect data. Data collection involves three distinct types, which are distinguished by the timeframe in which they are conducted. These are *baseline*, *formative*, and *summative* data collection. *Baseline* refers to data on outcomes that is collected before the project is implemented. *Formative* involves data on outcomes that is gathered while the project is underway. And *summative* refers to data on outcomes that is collected at the project's conclusion.

We have found that schools understand and have plenty of experience with collecting formative and summative data, but that far too many skip the step of collecting baseline data. In fact, we've visited schools with excellent service-learning or other innovative educational projects that were unable to demonstrate the full impact of the project because they failed to collect baseline data. Ultimately, gathering formative and summative data is both related to and dependent upon this initial process of baseline data collection.

The reason for this, put simply, is that it's difficult to measure the impact of a specific educational intervention over time without being able to describe where students (or the community or the school) actually started. It may be helpful to provide a hypothetical (if a bit absurd) illustration. At Grandparents' Day, most schools award a prize to the grandparent who traveled the farthest distance. In order to decide who gets the prize, the grandparents in attendance must know two things: (1) where they came from; and (2) approximately how far away their place of origin is. Can you imagine if, when asked, "Who traveled the farthest to get here?" grandparents all over the room raised their hands and commented about how long they felt the journey was, how it seemed to never end, and how exhausting it was? How could the bewildered principal at the front of the room determine who gets the prize for farthest distance traveled, without knowing the exact location of where people started?

While this example seems silly, the underlying principle applies to assessing service-learning projects. While it's helpful to gather participants' impressions of how the project went and how it affected them, it will be nearly impossible to determine the true impact without understanding what was going on before the project. True assessment of the project's impact necessarily involves some comparison of how far the classroom, school, and community have come as a result of the project. Thus, data collected throughout the project (formative assessment) and at the conclusion of the project (summative assessment) will need to be compared with baseline data to determine "how many miles" have been traveled as a result of the project.

Though sequencing data collection this way may sound difficult, it is relatively easy if the assessment table has been

Sample Assessment Table with Timeline

Area	Outcome	Instrumentation	Responsible Party/Resources	Timeline
Student Learning	Increased knowledge of course content	• Unit tests and course grades	• Classroom teacher; online course management system	**BASELINE:** Collect unit test grades and course grades during 1–2 years prior to implementing service-learning project **FORMATIVE:** Collect unit test grades during project (approx. every 4–6 weeks) **SUMMATIVE:** Collect course grades at conclusion of project year
		• Standardized testing	• Academic dean; standardized testing online results portal	**BASELINE:** Collect standardized testing results during 1–2 years prior to implementing service-learning project **FORMATIVE:** Collect during spring administration of project year **SUMMATIVE:** Access year-over-year comparisons, to be used in future data analysis

developed (as discussed in the preceding section). Essentially, all that needs to be done is to affix timeframes to the assessment table. We've depicted this using the same example (preceding page), for one of the outcomes previously identified (increased knowledge of course content, in the assessment area of student learning).

Although this is again a small slice showing how to map out one specific outcome in one area, it shows the level of forethought and detail that is needed to plan successfully for all three phases of assessment. It's also obvious that this map could get fairly long and unwieldy if too many outcomes have been identified for the project (which then require a similarly large number of assessments). This underscores the need for assessment of service-learning to be feasible, as discussed earlier.

Along these lines, more data is not always better when it comes to assessment. The best way to illustrate this is to use journals as an example. While we frequently see teachers who have used journals as a way to gauge student reflection in service-learning, the most successful teachers give highly structured journals—with specific prompts—and select only four to six over the course of the year to analyze. This still yields upwards of 100 pages for the teacher to grade via rubric and pull out salient quotes. (Five one-page journals, from 20 students in a class, equals 100 pages to analyze!) This is no small number, but it can be doable, especially if the teacher analyzes the data as it comes in. And, the data is more likely to be usable because the prompts elicit the data being sought (e.g., the ways students are connecting their academic learning in the classroom with the service experience, or what they are learning about being a part of God's restorative work in their communities). Contrast that with unstructured journals (without prompts) that are sampled two times per month, and that's easily 400 pages the teacher has to sift through in hopes of finding something insightful into students' learning and relative to the service-learning outcomes. Given this illustration, it's easy to see that *high-value* data is often better than *high-volume* data.

On a final note regarding data collection, it's important to remember that community-level data differs fundamentally from data collected at the school or classroom level. By and large, schools have considerable latitude when collecting data from and about their students, as long as the data sought can be connected directly to the educational process and isn't sensitive in nature (in which case, parental permission should be obtained prior to data collection). Community partners may have very different rules, however. For example, some partners may allow the constituents they serve to be surveyed (e.g., a senior citizen center), whereas confidentiality or logistics may prevent surveying those being served in some settings (e.g., a church food pantry). Thus, when seeking to collect data on community-level outcomes, schools and teachers should again seek to work with the community partner to determine how to best collect data—and to collect it collaboratively if at all possible.

Analyzing Data
How schools and teachers analyze data of course depends on the methods of data collection used. It is beyond the scope of this book to cover data analysis for every type of instrument, but we suggest some resources specific to each type (e.g.,

surveys, interviews, focus groups) in chapter 7. For the purposes of this chapter, however, there are a few points of guidance we can offer based on our experiences and research on best practices in assessment.

The first principle is to be as organized as possible while collecting data, so as to not misplace or lose data, or otherwise render it unusable. We have seen this all too often, and it most typically happens to teachers—who are already buried under mounds of paper (literally, or digitally). School leaders can help teachers in this regard by creating systems for collecting and depositing data along with clerical or administrative support. There are many free websites that allow for storing and sharing documents, some of which may already be in use at the school. We also have found that free online survey sites are useful for polling teachers throughout the year regarding their experiences, as well as keeping track of their progress in implementing their projects.

A second strategy for effective data analysis is to "analyze as you go." In the busyness of the school year it's easy to let data pile up as the weeks and months roll by, which makes for an unpleasant and often insurmountable summer project. It also means losing the opportunity to ask questions about the data as they arise during the year. Leaving those questions for the summer is too late, as most teachers are on break, and it will be hard to remember what happened the previous year once the new school year starts. One way to attack this issue is to create reports on service-learning outcomes at specific points of the year. This might be once a quarter or perhaps twice a year (at the midpoint and end). Reports should summarize how the project(s) have been implemented to date, what data have been collected, and an analysis of that data wherever possible. This formative analysis makes summative analysis much easier, as previous reports can be used to compile the final report. Regardless of the specifics, every school and teacher needs a data analysis plan—with time carved out to do the analysis—that is conducted throughout the academic year and not just at the end.

> **Service-Learning Snapshot:**
> To help lighten the end-of-the-year load for herself, an elementary school teacher working on a service-learning project on hydroponics and urban "food deserts" decided to gather and analyze data in real time, throughout the year. She collected copies of students' tests, journal entries, and other assessment measures immediately after they were completed. For quantitative data, she ran the basic calculations (averages, year-to-year comparisons, etc.) as soon as she had test data in hand. For the qualitative measures, she made sure the various documents she collected were collated and ready for analysis. She took pictures of her students using the hydroponics kits in the classroom, as well as volunteering with a local children's nutrition program that provided healthy lunch items to local schools. By the last day of school, she was ready to effortlessly hand over a box of data to her service-learning coordinator, making her close-out task list much shorter.

Finally, and perhaps most important, is the need to understand that making judgments about data from a mixed methods approach is different from most other approaches. Whereas in an experimental study it's relatively easy to tell whether or not an intervention worked (such as a new medicine in a clinical trial), there usually isn't a "smoking gun" when it comes to mixed methods. To help explain this to school leaders and teachers—who understandably want to know whether their projects "worked," given the substantial investment of time required—we often refer to Douglas Reeves' concept of the "jury effect." Although discussing action research projects, his concept is applicable to service-learning assessment (which, it can be argued, can often be considered a form of action research). In essence, juries make a "high stakes decision … based on the preponderance of evidence in a civil case or evidence beyond a reasonable doubt in a criminal case" (Reeves 2008, 35).

This is much the same approach that should be used when judging the data from a mixed-methods assessment of service-learning. With all the data analyzed, school leaders and teachers can make an informed judgment for each of the desired outcomes for service-learning in each of the three assessment areas (student learning and development, community impact, school improvement). This is most often accomplished by developing a narrative presentation of the data—in other words, telling the story of the project through data. This approach helps to make sense of each piece of data in light of the overall picture that emerges from all data sources.

This may seem like additional work, especially if it isn't required for external accountability purposes (e.g., by the school board, outside accrediting agency, or funder). However, this takes us back to the very purpose of assessment. Service-learning necessitates a significant investment of resources on the part of a school and its faculty, leaders, students, and community partners. In order to ensure those resources are being invested and stewarded wisely, it's crucial to assess whether service-learning is having a significant and positive impact on student learning and community needs. Without assessment, it's impossible to know for sure whether service-learning is making a difference, and how. And when properly analyzed, the data from assessment can provide valuable insight into how service-learning can be improved to have even greater impact, which leads to our final step in the assessment process.

Using Data to Make Adjustments
A comprehensive and accurate picture of the impact of service-learning is invaluable for making future adjustments. Certainly, no educational project or approach is perfect! School leaders and teachers should plan time to look at the service-learning assessment results and ask, "Now what?" This involves thinking about what changes need to be made to specific projects, implementation timelines, available resources, pedagogy, community partner arrangements, and even the assessment process itself.

Much like education, service-learning projects are "living": they are susceptible to many different variables and influences, all the way from the curriculum to the teacher's style to the characteristics of a given class of students. Even a major event like a hurricane or a snowstorm in any given year can disrupt scheduled service experiences, course content, exams, and so forth. All this is to say that "change is in the only constant" in education—and so too for service-learning. It's best to accept this up front and to even celebrate it, by viewing change as an opportunity for continuous improvement.

In our work with schools we've found that school leaders are generally more comfortable with this reality, but that teachers sometimes have a fear of their projects "failing." Once they've put together their project proposals, teachers will often ask questions like, "What if this doesn't work well? Do I have to stick with the same project each year?" Our response is always a resounding "No!" We do offer the caveat, though, that before throwing out the entire project, teachers should try to make changes to improve on the experience. Generally, teachers who have completed a year of service-learning—and who have good data on outcomes to examine—are committed to keeping their projects, and emerge confident about ways to make them even better for the following year.

Service-Learning Snapshot:
To ensure that data is used to inform instructional planning, a K–12 school engaged in service learning conducts an annual "data-dive" during a PD day. Faculty and administrators are divided into work groups based on various factors and are given access to different data sets, including standardized tests, class and school academic averages, etc. One of these groups looks explicitly at service-learning, by "diving" into the data looking for trends and patterns that may reflect the school's effectiveness in its service-learning initiatives. After processing what they discover, each group writes up a summary report along with recommendations for the administration team. In this way, the school's assessment of service-learning initiatives is grounded in data, which is augmented by further data collected from other varied assessment methods (such as surveys and analysis of student work products).

Finally, making adjustments to service-learning projects happens best when it is tied into regular change processes at the school. For example, teachers can be asked to think through changes to service-learning during their final supervisory meetings before summer break, or when they submit final course evaluations or feedback forms. Service-learning should be included as part of the regular curricular review cycle and process at schools. And strategic planning initiatives and evaluation can incorporate service-learning where appropriate, just as they would include instructional and programmatic activities. These efforts will help to integrate service-learning into the overall organizational learning processes of the school.

Next Steps

1. If you are a *teacher*, begin working on an assessment map (using the examples provided in this chapter) for a sample project and small set of outcomes for the project. List the kinds of assessment methods and tools you will use, being sure to note both existing sources of data you can access (e.g., parent surveys, standardized tests) as well as new ones you will need to identify or create.

2. If you are a *school leader*, begin working on an assessment map as described in step #1 above; however, focus on how you will guide and support assessment for multiple projects across different grade levels and/or departments.

Discussion Questions:

1. In general, does our school take a proactive, strategic approach to using data to inform instruction? How does the content of this chapter affirm or challenge our approach to data?

2. Why is assessing the outcomes of service-learning important to us, our classes, the school, and community partners we might work with?

3. What challenges might we face in assessing service-learning?

4. What resources might we need to identify in order to assess service-learning well?

7
Resources for Service-Learning

This final chapter identifies resources to support service-learning, including websites, organizations, and books that can inform service-learning project design (including identifying outcomes and conducting assessment), as well as templates we have used in working with teachers engaging in service-learning.

In this final chapter, we identify various organizations and guidebooks for K–12 service-learning that do not come from a uniquely Christian perspective, but that nonetheless may be helpful resources to Christian school educators. We also provide a list of books on research methodologies that may be useful in designing assessment for service-learning, as well as a list that has influenced our and many schools' thinking about outcomes of service-learning. Finally, we include a brainstorming worksheet and a report template to aid teachers and school leaders in developing and implementing service-learning projects.

It is our hope that along with the examples and case stories of service-learning provided throughout this book, school leaders and faculty will find inspiration to begin imagining their own projects with their own students. Along these same lines, we especially encourage Christian schools to connect with other schools engaged in service-learning. Whether through formal partnerships or informal networks, we've found that the greatest resource school leaders and teachers have—especially when it comes to implementing new ways of teaching and learning—is often each other. Shared PD, project idea exchanges, and partnerships to enact multischool projects are just some of the potential avenues for collaboration between schools. Working together across schools can provide the encouragement we deeply need as Christian educators and fellow believers (1 Thessalonians 5:11).

In closing, we firmly believe that service-learning is not only a promising pedagogy for achieving many of the unique aims of Christian education, but also an innovation for which Christian education is ready. While we pray this book is effective in helping schools start on the road to service-learning, we believe it is the larger learning community of Christian schools—working together—that can realize the potential of service-learning for God's restorative work, all to His glory.

Service-Learning Organizations and Websites

- **The National Service-Learning Clearinghouse** (https://gsn.nylc.org/clearinghouse) is a comprehensive library of service-learning resources for K–12 as well as higher education, which includes an online library of lesson plans, research, and project examples to support service-learning programs.

- **The National Youth Leadership Council** (https://nylc. org/) supports students, schools, and communities engaged together in service-learning. The site includes resources like the K–12 Service-Learning Standards for Quality Practice (shared in chapter 3 of this book), as well as the Generator School Network (a project planning tool and professional learning community for service-learning practitioners).

- **FFA's K–12 Service-Learning Project Planning Toolkit**, which includes the NYLC K–12 Service-Learning Standards for Quality Practice, is available for download for free at https://www.ffa.org/sitecollectiondocuments/lts_servicelearningtoolkit.pdf.

- **The Corporation for National and Community Service** (https://www.nationalservice.gov/) is a federal agency and grant maker that administers programs to engage Americans in service opportunities, including the Learn and Serve America program.

Service-Learning Guides

- ***The Complete Guide to Service Learning*** functions like a roadmap for service-learning and, like this guidebook, integrates the K–12 Service-Learning Standards for Quality Practice. One of the strengths of the book is that it offers a significant number of activities, ideas, book recommendations, and essays from experts in the field. Companion digital content is available and provides all planning and tracking forms referenced throughout the book. (Kaye, C. B. 2010. *The complete guide to service learning: Proven, practical ways to engage students in civic responsibility, academic curriculum, & social action.* 2nd ed. Minneapolis, MN: Free Spirit Publishing.)

- ***Learning Through Serving: A Student Guidebook for Service-Learning and Civic Engagement Across Academic Disciplines and Cultural Communities*** is written for both faculty and students involved in service-learning. The book includes sections on understanding service-learning, developing effective community partnerships, making meaning of out-of-the-classroom experiences, and assessing service-learning. One of the most notable features of this book is that it includes 60+ reflection exercises that can be adapted for diverse service-learning experiences (Collier, P. J., C. M. Cress, and V. L. Reitenauer. 2013. *Learning through serving: A student guidebook for service-learning and civic engagement across academic disciplines and cultural communities.* 2nd ed. Sterling, VA: Stylus Publishing.)

- ***Service Learning: A Guide to Planning, Implementing, and Assessing Student Projects*** breaks down service-learning planning and implementation processes into step-by-step instructions. The book also contains detailed plans for nine different service-learning projects (categorized as basic, intermediate, or advanced), accompanied by strategies for curricular alignment, tips for involving students, ideas for reflection exercises, and suggestions for differentiating service-learning for diverse learners. (Berman, S. 2015. *Service learning: A guide to planning, implementing, and assessing student projects.* 2nd ed. New York, NY: Skyhorse Publishing.)

- ***Change the World with Service Learning*** is a hands-on guide for teachers who want to integrate service-learning into their existing curriculum. This resource offers step-by-step instructions for how to plan and lead successful service-learning projects, and adds a section that captures the voices, reflections, and inspirations of teachers currently utilizing service-learning. (Farber, K. 2011. *Change the world with service learning: How to create, lead, and assess service learning projects.* Lanham, MD: Rowman & Littlefield Publishers.)

Assessment Resources

- Action research is an excellent methodology for assessing service-learning, and ***Action Research for School Leaders*** gives school leaders insight and understanding into how to harness the power of action research for school improvement. Practical steps are offered throughout the book, with topics including how to assemble an effective research team and analyze the data collected through action research. (Spaulding, D., and J. Falco. 2013. *Action research for school leaders.* Upper Saddle River, NJ: Pearson Education.)

- An influential and comprehensive guide for qualitative researchers, ***Qualitative Research & Evaluation Methods*** covers concepts related to how to choose appropriate qualitative research methods, how to design effective studies, and how to analyze qualitative data. The book need not be read from cover to cover in order for practitioners to benefit from it; for example, it can serve as a go-to resource for topics closely related to assessing service-learning, such as interviewing skills, effective questioning techniques, and leading effective group discussions. (Patton, M. Q. 2015. *Qualitative research & evaluation methods.* 4th ed. Thousand Oaks, CA: SAGE Publications, Inc.)

- Surveys are a common way to gather data related to the effectiveness of service-learning or to conduct needs assessment. ***The Survey Methods Workbook*** provides a comprehensive guide to crafting effective surveys, including extensive discussion about the appropriateness of surveys in various situations. Also, readers will find help for understanding and analyzing the qualitative and quantitative data that surveys can yield. (Buckingham, A., and P. Saunders. 2004. *The survey methods workbook.* Malden, MA: Polity Press.)

- Focus groups are a valuable and school-friendly methodology for understanding the impact of service-learning. ***Focus Groups: A Practical Guide for Applied Research*** provides information about how to effectively utilize focus groups, including offering a comprehensive overview of focus groups, planning effective group experiences, developing powerful questions, and analyzing data from focus groups. Of special interest to school leaders implementing service-learning are the chapters on focus group interviewing with young people and conducting focus groups cross-culturally. (Casey, M. A., and R.

A. Krueger. 2014. *Focus groups: A practical guide for applied research.* 5th ed. Thousand Oaks, CA: Sage Publications.)

Resources to Inform Service-Learning Outcomes

- *Where's the Learning in Service-Learning?* provides an overview of research on service-learning outcomes, as well as the history and theoretical basis for service-learning. This is a seminal book for both scholars and practitioners. Although written from a secular perspective, many of the service-learning outcomes identified in the book are congruent with the missions of Christian schools. (Eyler, J., and D. E. Giles. 1999. *Where's the learning in service-learning?* San Francisco: Jossey-Bass.)

- *Naming the Elephant: Worldview as a Concept*, a companion volume to Sire's *The Universe Next Door: A Basic Worldview Catalog*, provides a history and in-depth exploration of the concept of worldview. The book includes a brief discussion of worldviews in academic settings. (Sire, J. W. 2015. *Naming the elephant: Worldview as a concept.* 2nd. ed. Downers Grove, IL: Intervarsity Press.)

- *Worldview: The History of a Concept* traces the development of the concept of worldview across time, Christian traditions, and the academic disciplines of the natural and social sciences. (Naugle, D. K. 2002. Worldview: *The history of a concept.* Grand Rapids, MI: Wm. B. Eerdmans Publishing Co.)

- **Teaching Redemptively** examines the role of teachers as God's image-bearers and discusses how teachers can "teach redemptively" by employing biblical principles throughout their work. In particular, Graham lays out the biblical narrative as a framework for building educational practice. (Graham, D. L. 2009. *Teaching redemptively: Bringing grace and truth into your classroom.* 2nd ed. Colorado Springs, CO: Purposeful Design Publications.)

- **To Change the World** provides a paradigm for Christian living at both the individual and institutional levels, namely "faithful presence," which can inform Christian educators' understanding of the aims of Christian schooling and the ways they teach and learn. (Hunter, J. D. 2010. *To change the world: The irony, tragedy, and possibility of Christianity in the late modern world.* New York: Oxford University Press.)

- **You Are What You Love: The Spiritual Power of Habit** lays out a vision of spiritual formation as being mediated by cultural liturgies—either a myriad of secular ones, or that of Christian orthodoxy. In addition to the model of human flourishing presented in the book, a section on teaching for formation is valuable for Christian educators. (Smith, J. K. A. 2016. *You are what you love: The spiritual power of habit.* Grand Rapids, MI: Brazos Press.)

- **Visions of Vocation: Common Grace for the Common Good** discusses the Christian's calling and relationship with the world, in terms of recovering a vision of vocation that centers on love and restoration. It addresses the larger question of "purpose" that often arises in contexts like the Christian school. (Garber, S. 2014. *Visions of vocation: Common grace for the common good*. Downers Grove, IL: InterVarsity Press.)

- ***Restoring All Things*** emphasizes the restorative role of Christian organizations that function in the "middle" between the individual and the government. These organizations include schools, associations, parachurch ministries, churches, and families. Besides a compelling vision for active partnership with God in bringing the reality of His kingdom to bear on earth, the book features stories of people who are living out that vision in very practical ways, which can encourage Christian schools to find their own ways to practice restoration. (Smith, C. S., and J. Stonestreet. 2015. *Restoring all things: God's audacious plan to change the world through everyday people*. Grand Rapids, MI: Baker Books.)

BRAINSTORMING SERVICE-LEARNING PROJECTS: A WORKSHEET FOR FACULTY

Brainstorm a potential service-learning project for a specific grade level and subject area at your school. Briefly describe it here:

Now, list considerations for the following questions:

1. How would the project link to the curriculum? (Think of specific units, topics, etc.)

2. Identify 5–6 student outcomes for the project. (Outcomes should be diverse and include academic, worldview, personal development, and other domains.)

3. What specific service experiences might be part of the project? (Aim for 3–4 over the year.)

4. How would the school/class connect with the community (a church, agency, group, etc.) to make the project happen?

5. How can student reflection be incorporated into the project?

6. What budgeting, transportation, or other logistical issues would need to be considered?

7. What support would the teacher need from administration to make the project successful?

8. How could the student outcomes (from question 2) be assessed? How would you know (what evidence would you accept) that students achieved those outcomes?

SERVICE-LEARNING PROGRESS REPORT
QUARTER (circle): **1 2 3 4**

1. Faculty Name(s) _____

2. In just a few words, describe what your class did this past quarter in terms of service-learning.

3. In general, on average, how much time did your class spend each week on service-learning? (Feel free to answer in hours, class periods, days, etc.—whatever is the easiest for you.)

4. Briefly describe the learning that your students experienced as a result of participating in your project. Please include attainment of learning outcomes identified for the project, which should encompass multiple domains (i.e., academic, worldview, personal development, and other domains).

5. List and briefly describe the service activities your students participated in this past quarter for service-learning. Also provide the day and date of the activity.

6. Identify four measures (ideally two quantitative—e.g., tests/grades; plus two qualitative—e.g., papers, project, journals, etc.) that you collected from the last school year that you are collecting *again* this year, to compare how your students performed. Next to each one, indicate whether this year's data has been collected yet.

	Collected yet this year? (circle)
1. Measure: _____	YES / NO
2. Measure: _____	YES / NO
3. Measure: _____	YES / NO
4. Measure: _____	YES / NO

7. List below the total dollar amount of expenditures for your service-learning project (that were paid by the school) in the past quarter, as well as the amount contributed by students (e.g., for busing).

School Expenditure: $ _____

Student Expenditure: $ _____

8. Describe the greatest challenge you faced in implementing service-learning in the past quarter.

9. What are you planning to do to move your project forward in this quarter?

10. Provide any additional feedback (or comments on your answers above) that you'd like to share at this point.

References

Astin, A. W., L. J. Sax, and J. Avalos. 1999. Long-term effects of volunteerism during the undergraduate years. *Review of Higher Education* 22 no. 2: 187–202.

Bain, J. D., R. Ballantyne, C. Mills, and N. C. Lester. 2002. *Reflecting on practice: Student teachers' perspectives.* Flaxton, Queensland, Australia: Post Pressed.

Berson, J. S., and W. F. Younkin. 1998. Doing well by doing good: A study of the effects of a service-learning experience on student success. Paper presented at the American Society of Higher Education, Miami, FL.

Carver, R. 1997. Theoretical underpinnings of service-learning. *Theory into Practice* 36 no. 3: 143–149.

Colby, A., T. Ehrlich, E. Beaumont, and J. Stephens. 2003. *Educating citizens: Preparing America's undergraduates for lives of moral and civic responsibility.* San Francisco: Jossey-Bass.

Erdvig, R. C. S. 2016. A model for worldview development in evangelical Christian emerging adults. Doctoral dissertation. Liberty University, Lynchburg, VA.

Eyler, J., and D. E. Giles, Jr. 1999. *Where's the learning in service-learning?* San Francisco: Jossey-Bass.

Farber, K. 2011. *Change the world with service learning: How to organize, lead, and assess service-learning projects.* Lanham, MA: Rowman & Littlefield Publishers, Inc.

Felten, P., and P. Clayton. 2011. Service-learning. *New Directions for Teaching and Learning* 128:75–84.

Fowler, J. W. 2000. *Becoming adult, becoming Christian: Adult development and Christian faith.* San Francisco: Jossey-Bass Publishers.

Furco, A., and S. Root. 2010. Research demonstrates the value of service learning. *Phi Delta Kappan* 91 no. 5: 16–20.

Garber, S. 2007. *The fabric of faithfulness: Weaving together belief and behavior.* Downers Grove, IL: InterVarsity Press.

---. 2014. *Visions of vocation: Common grace for the common good.* Downers Grove, IL: InterVarsity Press.

Graham, D. L. 2009. *Teaching redemptively: Bringing grace and truth into your classroom.* 2nd ed. Colorado Springs, CO: Purposeful Design Publications.

Hambrick, J. 2016. *Move toward the mess: The ultimate fix for a boring Christian life.* Colorado Springs, CO: David C. Cook.

Hull, J.E. 2003. Aiming for Christian education, settling for Christians educating: The Christian school's replication of a public school paradigm. *Christian Scholar's Review* 32 no. 2: 203-223.

Hunter, J.D. 2010. T*o change the world: The irony, tragedy, and possibility of Christianity in the late modern world.* Oxford: Oxford University Press.

Jacoby, B. 1996. Service-learning in today's higher education. In *Service-learning in higher education: Concepts and practices,* ed. B. Jacoby and associates, 3–25. San Francisco: Jossey-Bass.

Kaye, C. 2004. *The complete guide to service-learning.* Minneapolis, MN: Free Spirit Publishing.

Kielsmeier, J. 2011. Service-learning: The time is now. *The Prevention Researcher* 18 no. 1: 3–7.

Koltko-Rivera, M. E. 2004. The psychology of worldviews. *Review of General Psychology.* 8 no. 1: 3–58.

Myers-Lipton, S. J. 1998. Effect of a comprehensive service-learning program on college students' civic responsibility. *Teaching Sociology* 26 no. 4: 243–58.

National Youth Leadership Council. 2008. *K–12 service-learning standards for quality practice.* St. Paul, MN: Authors.

Pearcy, N. 2004. *Total truth: Liberating Christianity from its cultural captivity.* Wheaton, IL: Crossway Books.

Phillips, W. G., W. E. Brown, and J. Stonestreet. 2008. *Making sense of your world: A biblical worldview.* 2nd ed. Salem, WI: Sheffield.

Prentice, M. 2007. Service learning and civic engagement. *Academic Questions* 20 no. 2: 135–145.

Radecke, M. W. 2007. Service-learning and faith formation. *Journal of College and Character* 8 no. 5: 1–28.

Rama, D. V., S. P. Ravenscroft, S. K. Wolcott, and E. Zlotkowski. 2000. Service-learning outcomes: Guidelines for educators and researchers. *Issues in Accounting Education* 15 no. 4: 657–692.

Reeves, D. B. 2008. *Reframing teacher leadership to improve your school.* Alexandria, VA: ASCD.

Schultz, K. G., and J. A. Swezey. 2013. A three-dimensional concept of worldview. *Journal of Research on Christian Education* 22 no. 3: 227–243.

Sire, J. W. 1997. *The universe next door: A basic worldview catalog.* 4th ed. Downers Grove, IL: Intervarsity Press.

---. 2015. *Naming the elephant: Worldview as a concept.* 2nd. ed. Downers Grove, IL: Intervarsity Press.

Smith, J. K. A. 2009. *Desiring the kingdom: Worship, worldview, and cultural formation.* Grand Rapids: Baker Academic.

Stanton, T. K., D. E. Giles Jr., and N. I. Cruz. 1999. *Service-learning: A movement's pioneers reflect on its origins, practice, and future.* San Francisco: Jossey-Bass.

Swaner, L. E. 2016. *Professional development for Christian school educators and leaders: Frameworks and best practices.* Colorado Springs, CO: Association of Christian Schools International.

———. 2016a. Needs assessment for strategic planning. In A. Pue, *Rethinking strategic planning for Christian schools*, 192–222. Colorado Springs, CO: Purposeful Design Publications.

Swaner, L., and J. Brownell. 2008. *Outcomes of high-impact practices for underserved students: A review of the literature.* Washington, DC.: Association of American Colleges and Universities.

Swaner, L., and R. C. S. Erdvig. 2018. *K–12 supplemental service-learning standards for Christian education settings.* Smithtown, NY: Authors.

Twenge, J.M. 2017. *iGen: Why today's super-connected kids are growing up less rebellious, more tolerant, less happy--and completely unprepared for adulthood.* New York: Atria Books.

Valk, J. 2013. Christianity through a worldview lens. *Journal of Adult Theological Education* 9 no. 2: 158–174.

Vogelgesang, L. J., and A. W. Astin. 2000. Comparing the effects of community service and service-learning. *Michigan Journal of Community Service Learning* no. 7: 25–34.

Warren, J. 2012. Does service-learning increase student learning? A meta-analysis. *Michigan Journal of Community Service Learning* 18 no. 2: 56–61.

White, A. 2001. A meta-analysis of service learning research in middle and high schools. Doctoral dissertation. University of North Texas, Denton, TX.